MARK
The Serving Christ

The Son of Man did not come to be served, but to serve,
and to give His life as a ransom for many.
Mark 10:45

By Julene Gernant Dumit

CPH
SAINT LOUIS

Series editors: Thomas J. Doyle and Rodney L. Rathmann

Assistant to the editors: Cynthia Anderson

We solicit your comments and suggestions concerning this material. Please write to Product Manager, Adult Bible Studies, Concordia Publishing House, 3558 South Jefferson Avenue, St. Louis, MO 63118-3968.

1   2   3   4   5   6   7   8   9   10   05   04   03   02   01   00   99   98   97   96

Contents

Preface

The aim of this study is to get you into the Bible. It is not a commentary. It is a guide to help you master this gospel. It teaches you how to use your Bible. It is not a study about the Bible; it is a study of the Bible.

Follow these three steps in your study of this gospel or any other portion of the Bible.

1. Observe: *What does it say?* Get at the exact meaning of the text. Never read what isn't there. Observe accurately what is on the page; read as though you had never seen it before.

2. Interpret: *What does it mean?* Be sure that you always let the Bible be its own interpreter. Make use of the cross references if your Bible has them.

3. Apply: *What does it mean to me?* God has a message for me today. What am I to believe? to do? to be? How am I to live? What does the text say about the world in which I live today?

Study it through! Write it down! Pray it in! Pass it on! Live it out!

Read Mark often during the time of this course. Repeated reading gains for you more than anything else you can do.

Read with special attention the chapter to be discussed at your next class session; note the questions you want to ask and the points you wish to share.

You are also encouraged to use the Bible dictionaries, Bible helps, study Bibles, and commentaries that you have available to enrich your study. Read them before class, bring them to class to refer to, and use them in private study to gain insights that you can share with the whole class.

Also make Mark the subject of your personal devotional reading. Read a short section until you come to something especially meaningful to you. Stop to meditate on it. Follow this pattern:

1. What is God giving me? Doctrine? Counsel? Comfort? Warning? Courage? A principle to live by?

2. Find in it thanks, praise, confession, or something to intercede for, and turn the passage into a prayer.

3. Resolve to believe, to do, or to be what the passage has told you. Ask for and rely on the Holy Spirit's power and guidance to enable you.

May God bless you as you study. May His Spirit work through this Word to strengthen your faith, deepen your appreciation of God's gift of life and salvation, and help you to rededicate yourselves to lives of love and service.

Lesson 1

Jesus Begins His Ministry (Mark 1)

Theme Verse

"The beginning of the gospel about Jesus Christ, the Son of God" (**Mark 1:1**).

Goal

We seek to learn about Mark and what he wrote about the start of Jesus' ministry.

What's Going On Here?

What do you know about the Mark who wrote this gospel? Since he was not an eyewitness to most of the events he recorded, where did he get his information? The first part of this lesson will address these questions.

Mark, the shortest of the gospels, records nothing about Jesus' birth or early life, but begins with the ministry of John the Baptist. We will look at what Mark recorded about John, about Jesus' Baptism and temptation, about the call of the first disciples, and about Jesus' authority to teach and heal and drive out demons.

Searching the Scriptures

Early church writings from the second century tell us that the author of this gospel was Mark and that Mark was a close associate of Peter from whose preaching Mark received the information recorded in this gospel.

1. It is generally agreed that this Mark is the person mentioned in **Acts 12:12, 25; 13:4–5, 13; 15:36–40; Colossians 4:10; 2 Timothy 4:11.** What information is given in these verses about him?

12:12 John MARK, House.

13:4-5 Help mission Afro.

4:10 MARK WAS CAUSE with BARNBAS

4:11 Suport For APOSALS

2. How did Peter express his close relationship to Mark in **1 Peter 5:13?** *Son*

Note also in **1 Peter 5:13** the mention of Babylon, which many scholars think is a symbolic reference to Rome. According to tradition, Peter was in Rome during the last years of his life and there suffered martyrdom during the persecution of Christians by the Roman emperor Nero.

Early church documents indicate that the gospel of **Mark** was written in Rome. It has been suggested by some scholars that Mark wrote his gospel for the Christians at Rome who were undergoing the terrible Neronian persecution (which took place about A.D. 64–67), seeking to strengthen them by holding before them the life of Jesus.

Mark is the shortest of the gospels, recording more of what Jesus did than what He said. A verse that neatly summarizes Jesus' mission is **Mark 10:45.** If you have never done so, you would do well to memorize this verse. Scan the section titles throughout the book, and note Jesus' acts of service and the offering up of His life as a ransom for many.

3. Read **Mark 1:1**, which appears to be a title for the entire book. The word *beginning* echoes **Genesis 1:1**, "In the beginning God created the heavens and the earth." Here, **Mark** tells us, God was making a new beginning. What does **Mark** record the beginning of? If this is only the beginning, what is the continuation and the ending?

4. Read **Mark 1:2–8.** What was John the Baptist's relationship to the Old Testament prophecies quoted by Mark? What was John's role? How did he carry it out? What was his message **(1:7–8)?**

He was A messenger   with water

5. Read **1:9–13.** Although He did not need to repent and receive forgiveness, Jesus came from Nazareth to be baptized by John. He did so as the substitute for sinful humanity. His baptism was also His inauguration into ministry. How did God the Father place His stamp of approval on Jesus and His work (see **Psalm 2:7; Isaiah 42:1**)? How was Jesus empowered for that work? What was His first battle on behalf of sinful humanity? Devil

6. Read **Mark 1:14–20.** God's people were expecting the coming of the kingdom that was to be inaugurated by the promised Messiah. What was Jesus' message about the kingdom **(1:15)?** What kind of radical choice did people have to make if they wanted to participate in the coming kingdom with joy?

7. Jesus' call to come and follow Him, the call to discipleship, was an urgent call, one that demanded an immediate response. How did the response of Peter, Andrew, James, and John show that Jesus should take precedence over everything else? What did Jesus promise to make them?

Familys, JoBs.   *Fishers of men*

8. Read **1:21–28.** The other rabbis of Jesus' time taught by quoting the opinions of other rabbis. How did Jesus show His authority as the Son of God? How did even the demon acknowledge that? What was the reaction of the people to Jesus? *Amazement*

2 Tought with Athorty.

9. Read **1:29–34.** How did Jesus respond to the sick or demon possessed who were brought to Him? How did Peter's mother-in-law show her gratitude?   *Healed them. She waited on them.*

10. Read **1:35–39.** Early the next morning, after a busy evening of healing and casting out demons, what did Jesus do? While people were looking for Jesus because of His miracles, what did Jesus say was the reason for His coming **(1:38)?** *(Prayed) To preach*

11. Read **1:40–45.** How did the leprous man express his faith in Jesus? How did Jesus treat him? Why do you think Jesus was so concerned that the man not tell anyone? What happened as a result of the man not obeying Jesus? *(you can make me clean.) To get up AND preach.*

The Word for Us

1. What does Jesus teach us about prayer? See **Mark 1:35.**

Prayer is very importen

2. Even though Jesus doesn't call many present-day disciples to leave their homes, families, and occupations, He still wants to have first place in their lives. In what ways can we give Him that place?

Setting time Aside time.
Reading Bible.

3. Jesus calls all who would follow Him to be fishers of people. How are we fishers? *To preach the word.*

4. What can the result of the leprous man's disobedience teach us about disobeying Jesus even with the best of intentions?

Closing

Sing or read together the following stanzas of "Oh, Love, How Deep."

Oh, love, how deep, how broad, how high,
Beyond all thought and fantasy,
That God, the Son of God, should take
Our mortal form for mortal's sake!

For us baptized, for us He bore
His holy fast and hungered sore;
For us temptation sharp He knew;
For us the tempter overthrew.

For us He prayed; for us He taught;
For us His daily works He wrought,
By words and signs and actions thus
Still seeking not Himself but us.

To Do This Week

As noted in the introduction, you will benefit from reading through the entire gospel several times. For next time, pay particular attention to **Mark 2–3.**

Lesson 2

Jesus Receives Acclaim and Opposition (Mark 2-3)

Theme Verse

Jesus said to them, "It is not the healthy who need a doctor, but the sick. I have not come to call the righteous, but sinners" **(Mark 2:17).**

Goal

We seek to learn how Jesus dealt with those who sought His healing, as well as those who opposed it.

What's Going On Here?

As Jesus' preaching and healing ministry progressed, it drew much attention. On the one hand, Jesus was often surrounded by crowds who sought to be taught and healed by Him. They were the spiritually and physically sick who recognized their sickness and their need for the healing Jesus brought. On the other hand, religious leaders cast a critical eye on what Jesus was doing and saying. They were righteous in their own eyes and saw no need for Jesus' healing. In this lesson we will look at how Jesus dealt with both groups of people.

Searching the Scriptures

Read **2:1–12.** Apparently Jesus made Capernaum His home after being driven out of Nazareth **(Luke 4:14–31).** It is reasonable to think that He may have lived at the home of Peter and Andrew. When He returned home, many people gathered to Him and He preached the word to them.

The typical house of that time had a flat roof that could be easily reached by a staircase on the outside of the building. The roof often consisted of wooden beams on which were laid mats of branches over which was packed a thick layer of clay.

1. What did the persistent actions of the men in digging through the roof and lowering their friend before Jesus say about them? What did Jesus say to the paralytic? Why do you think He said that?

2. Among the crowd were teachers of the law, experts in the written Law of God and its oral interpretation. They questioned Jesus' authority to forgive sins. In what way were their assumptions right? In what way were they wrong?

Jesus knew what they were thinking and challenged them by asking which was easier: to announce forgiveness or to tell the man to get up and walk. Both actions could only be accomplished by God or those to whom He had granted the authority and power. But the teachers of the law probably thought that it was easier to announce forgiveness since there was no way to verify that. By healing the man, Jesus showed that He had the authority to heal and by implication that He also had the authority to forgive sins.

To those with eyes to see, Jesus' healing miracles reinforced His preaching that the messianic kingdom (reign) of God, foretold in the Old Testament, was near.

> The healing of the paralytic was more than a display of mercy to a wretched man. The announcement and presentation of radical healing to a man in his entire person was a sign of the Kingdom of God drawn near. The paralytic experienced the fulfillment of God's promise that the lame

would share in the joy of the coming salvation (Isa. 35:6; Jer. 31:8). The demonstration that God had come near to his people was startling. All present [including the teachers of the law] glorified God because he redeemed men from every distress (William L. Lane, *The Gospel According to Mark*, The New International Commentary on the New Testament [Grand Rapids, MI: Eerdmans, 1974], p. 99).

3. Read **Mark 2:13–17.** What objection to Jesus did the teachers of the law voice here? Why? How did Jesus respond?

As Lane in his commentary points out, something far more radical than what the Pharisees realized was going on at Levi's house:

When Jesus shared meal fellowship with the tax officials and the common people, it was Messiah who was sitting with sinners. The expression used in [Mark] 2:15, "they reclined at table together with Jesus," suggests that Jesus—the Messiah—and not Levi, was the host at this festive meal. When this is understood, the interest of the entire pericope centers on the significance of Messiah eating with sinners. The specific reference in verse 17 to Jesus' call of sinners to the Kingdom suggests that the basis of table-fellowship was *messianic forgiveness*, and the meal itself was an anticipation of the messianic banquet. When Jesus broke bread with the outcasts, Messiah ate with them at his table and extended to them fellowship with God. ... The meal was an extension of the grace of God and an anticipation of the consummation when Messiah will sit down with sinners in the Kingdom of God (pp. 106–7).

4. Read **2:18–22.** What point was Jesus making in His response to the question about fasting?

5. Read **2:23–28.** How did Jesus correct the Pharisees' understanding of the Sabbath? What did He proclaim about Himself? What implications did this have?

6. Read **3:1–6.** What is the answer to the question Jesus asked in **3:4** (see **Hosea 6:6**)? Why didn't the Pharisees answer? Why was Jesus angry and deeply distressed? How did the Pharisees further display their hardness of heart? Why?

Read **3:7–12.** Note that the demons' statement is not a confession of faith but an acknowledgement of who Jesus is—the Son of God.

Read **3:13–19.** Just as God's Old Testament people began as the 12 sons of Jacob, so the new people of God that Jesus was forming would begin with 12. Thus while Jesus was building a new community, His choice of *12* apostles shows the continuity between this new community and God's Old Testament people. See **Revelation 21:9–14.**

7. What special experience were these 12 to have? What do you think was the benefit of that experience? What was to be their mission?

Read **3:20–30.** Here we see two more instances where Jesus faced opposition. Hearing that He was not even taking time to eat, His family concluded that He must be out of His mind and went to take charge of Him. And the teachers of the law attempted to explain His ability to drive out demons by saying that He did so with Satan's power.

8. Jesus responded to the teachers of the law with three points. What point did Jesus make in **3:23–26?** To what was Jesus referring in **3:27?**

9. What sin were the teachers of the law committing or in danger of committing **(3:28–30)?** Of what does this sin consist? Why is it unforgivable? Could those who worry about having committed it possibly have done so?

10. Read **3:31–35.** Who are Jesus' family members?

The Word for Us

1. In what ways does or can your church exhibit the radical nature of the forgiveness and fellowship with God that Jesus brings?

2. The 12 apostles learned discipleship by being with Jesus. How do we learn what it means to be disciples?

Closing

Sing or read together the following stanzas of "My Song Is Love Unknown":

> My song is love unknown,
>> My Savior's love to me,
> Love to the loveless shown
>> That they might lovely be.
> Oh, who am I
>> That for my sake
>> My Lord should take
> Frail flesh and die?
>
> He came from His blest throne
>> Salvation to bestow;
> But men made strange, and none
>> The longed-for Christ would know.
> But, oh, my friend,
>> My friend indeed,
>> Who at my need
> His life did spend!
>
> Here might I stay and sing,
>> No story so divine!
> Never was love, dear King,
>> Never was grief like Thine.
> This is my Friend,
>> In whose sweet praise
>> I all my days
> Could gladly spend!

To Do This Week

As noted in the introduction, you will benefit from reading through the entire gospel several times. For next time, pay particular attention to **Mark 4–5.**

Lesson 3

The Secret of the Kingdom (Mark 4–5)

Theme Verses

"When [Jesus] was alone, the Twelve and the others around Him asked Him about the parables. He told them, 'The secret of the kingdom of God has been given to you. But to those on the outside everything is said in parables' " **(Mark 4:10–11).**

Goal

We seek to learn what the secret of the kingdom is, to whom it is revealed, and from whom it is hidden. We also seek to understand what is taught about the kingdom in parables and why Jesus used parables. And we seek to understand how Jesus' miracles provide further evidence to support the secret of the kingdom.

What's Going On Here?

In the previous lesson, we saw that responses to Jesus can take one of two forms: faith or opposition. In this lesson we will see what that means for each group of people with regard to the kingdom of God and the secret about kingdom that Jesus came to reveal. We will look at Jesus' teachings about the kingdom and at how Jesus displayed His power as Lord and as Savior.

Searching the Scriptures

Read **4:1–9.** Mark recorded that Jesus taught many things in parables. Truth is conveyed in a parable using concrete pictures rather than abstractions. When we attempt to make a point, we sometimes use figurative language to illustrate the point, but usually the main thrust of our point is made with abstract language. In contrast, parables use figurative language as the main vehicle that conveys the meaning. Parables engage the imagination. They are meant to provoke thought about the point being made and often require effort to understand. The picture language involves the hearers in the situation and challenges them to apply what is being taught to themselves.

1. What did Jesus exhort the people to do in **4:3?** According to **4:9,** what is necessary to do this?

2. Read **4:10–12.** What is the secret of the kingdom of God? To whom has the secret been revealed? From whom is it hidden?

So we see that a necessary ingredient for properly understanding the parables is faith. To those who refuse to believe, the parables remain obscure. Parables have the double function of teaching those who are willing to learn and keeping the secret hidden from those who would only scorn it. We have seen these two responses to Jesus previously in **Mark,** and they are illustrated in the parable of the sower.

3. Read Jesus' explanation of the parable in **4:13–20.** What is the word that the farmer sows? What things hinder that word from taking root and producing fruit in people's lives? What is illustrated by the seed that falls on fertile soil?

Read **4:21–23.** Although Jesus' identity is revealed now only to the eyes of faith, it will not remain hidden forever. This parable looks to the end of history when Jesus will be revealed in all His glory to everyone.

4. Read **4:24–25.** In this parable Jesus addresses how we make use of the Word He has sown in our lives. How are we encouraged to use that Word in rich measure, that is believe it, let it transform our lives, and share it with others? What is in store for those who neglect that Word?

5. Read **4:26–29.** What happens between when the seed (the Gospel) is sown and the harvest? Where does the power that produces that result lie? What is the role of the sower?

6. Read **4:30–34.** What comparison is made in the parable? What does that teach us about the kingdom of God?

7. Read **4:35–41.** How did Jesus still the storm? Why did He rebuke the disciples? What was revealed about Jesus in the stilling of the storm?

8. Read **5:1–20.** How did the demons acknowledge Jesus' superior power? What do the condition of the man while being possessed and what happened to the swine say about the intent of the demons?

9. In contrast to how the people of the region responded to the miracle, how did the healed man respond? What did Jesus instruct the man to do? How did the man comply?

10. Read **5:21–34.** Jairus approached Jesus with complete faith that Jesus could heal his daughter. The woman too approached Jesus with complete faith, but she seems to have entertained an almost magical notion of how Jesus' power worked. How did Jesus' words to her clarify what had happened? Of what did Jesus assure her?

11. Read **5:35–43.** After hearing that the girl had died, what did Jesus call Jairus to do? Jesus had previously shown Himself master over sin, disease, and Satan and his forces. Over what enemy of all people did Jesus show Himself as conqueror in this incident? Who was allowed to witness this display? Who was specifically put out of the house beforehand? Again, what point about the secret of the kingdom was made by this exclusion?

The Word for Us

1. The parable of the sower not only speaks to people's initial reception of the Gospel, but how it takes root and produces fruit throughout their lives. What things should we beware of and for what things should we pray that the Gospel might produce a bountiful harvest in our lives?

2. What do the parable of the sower and the parable of the growing seed **(4:26–29)** teach us about our responsibility for the seed?

3. At the end of his discussion of Jesus stilling the storm, William Lane says this:

> The subduing of the sea and the wind was not merely a demonstration of power; it was an epiphany, through which Jesus was unveiled to his disciples as the Savior in the midst of intense peril. Very early this incident was understood as a sign of Jesus' saving presence in the persecution which threatened to overwhelm the Church. It is not surprising that in early Christian art the Church was depicted as a boat driven upon a perilous sea; with Jesus in the midst, there was nothing to fear (*The Gospel of Mark*, The New International Commentary on the New Testament [Grand Rapids, MI: Eerdmans, 1974], p. 178).

Talk about the comfort this provides you as an individual and the church at large and in what circumstances.

4. Talk about what aspects of Jesus' Lordship (His power over nature, Satan, sin, disease, or death) are most comforting to you and at what times.

Closing

Sing or read together the following stanza of "I Know My Faith Is Founded":

> Increase my faith, dear Savior,
>> For Satan seeks by night and day
> To rob me of this treasure
>> And take my hope of bliss away.
> But, Lord, with You beside me,
>> I shall be undismayed;
> And led by Your good Spirit,
>> I shall be unafraid.
> Abide with me, O Savior,
>> A firmer faith bestow;
> Then I shall bid defiance
>> To ev'ry evil foe.

To Do This Week

As noted in the introduction, you will benefit from reading through the entire gospel several times. For next time, pay particular attention to **Mark 6–7.**

Lesson 4

A Prophet Is Often without Honor (Mark 6–7)

Theme Verse

"Jesus said to them, 'Only in his hometown, among his relatives and in his own house is a prophet without honor' " **(Mark 6:4).**

Goal

We seek to understand who Jesus revealed Himself to be and why that did not bring Him the honor He deserved.

What's Going On Here?

A prophet is accorded no honor in his hometown. But as we will see in this lesson, that doesn't mean that he is universally acclaimed elsewhere. In this lesson we will read about the death of John the Baptist, about the disciples' failure to respond to Jesus in faith, and about Jesus' continuing controversy with the religious leaders. All of this is in stark contrast with the honor accorded Him by a Gentile woman and by His deeds that should have brought Him complete honor as the Son of God.

Searching the Scriptures

1. Read **6:1–6a.** Although **Mark** doesn't specifically say so, this incident seems to have taken place in Nazareth. It is most likely a different incident than the one recorded in **Luke 4.** What kept the people from believing that Jesus' authority and power were from God? What kept Jesus from doing

many miracles among them?

2. Read **6:6b–13.** Jesus commissioned the Twelve to a specific task. The instructions that He gave were operative for that specific, temporary assignment and were not meant to be permanent. How did Jesus extend His ministry through the Twelve? Upon whom were the disciples forced to depend as they carried out their assignment? What message were the disciples to give those who rejected them?

3. Read **6:14–29.** Herod Antipas, a son of Herod the Great, was ruler of Galilee and Perea, a strip of land east of the Jordan River near the Dead Sea. What speculations about Jesus' identity were circulating in Galilee? Why would Herod's belief about who Jesus was be particularly disturbing to him? Why was John killed?

4. Read **6:30–44.** Why did Jesus have compassion on the people **(6:34)?** What did that prompt Him to do? How did the disciples show that they still did not fully understand who Jesus was? What did the inventory of available supplies show? What parallels can you find between this account and **Exodus 16:1–3, 11–15?**

5. Read **6:45–56.** If the disciples had understood about the loaves, they would have been prepared for their next amazing encounter with Jesus, but they had not. Why not **(6:51–52)?** To those familiar with such Old Testament passages as **Isaiah 41:10, 13; 43:1–2; Job 9:8; Psalm 77:19,** what do Jesus' words and His walking on the water indicate?

6. Read **Mark 7:1–23.** What uncleanness is God concerned about? Why? What kind of obedience pleases Him?

Read **7:24–30.** Jesus' mission while He was on earth was directed toward the people of Israel, as He told this woman in part of their dialog recorded in **Matthew 15:24** but not here in **Mark.** In order to prepare the right conditions for the coming of the Savior, God had chosen Abraham and his descendants to be His people and to receive His revelation. It was to them, whom God had carefully prepared, that the Messiah, Jesus, came. It was only after Jesus' death, resurrection, and ascension that God widened the scope of His salvation to include the whole world, something that He had planned from eternity.

But this woman, who wanted Jesus to step outside of the bounds of His ministry, exhibited something in great contrast to Israel's religious leaders and even to the disciples whose hearts remained hard after the feeding of the five thousand.

7. What did this woman exhibit? How? How did Jesus respond?

8. Read **7:31–37.** Then read **Isaiah 35:4–6** which records the Old Testament promise that Jesus fulfilled in the healing of this man. Again Jesus tried to stop the spread of the news about what He had done because He did not want to be known merely as a miracle worker. But it was to no avail. What did the people confess about Him?

The Word for Us

1. What meaning would the account of the death of John the Baptist have had for those experiencing persecution at the hand of Nero? What does it tell us about the cost of following the Lord?

2. There is both a now and a not-yet aspect to the kingdom of God. In Jesus' healing miracles we see a glimpse of the physical as well as spiritual healing that Jesus came to bring. According to **Revelation 21:1–4,** when will complete wholeness be a reality for us?

Closing

Sing or read together the following stanza of "What God Ordains Is Always Good":

> What God ordains is always good:
> >   This truth remains unshaken.
> Though sorrow, need, or death be mine,
> >   I shall not be forsaken.
> I fear no harm,
> For with His arm
> He shall embrace and shield me;
> So to my God I yield me.

To Do This Week

As noted in the introduction, you will benefit from reading through the entire gospel several times. For next time, pay particular attention to **Mark 8:1–9:13.**

Lesson 5

The Christ Must Suffer (Mark 8:1–9:13)

Theme Verse

"[Jesus] then began to teach them that the Son of Man must suffer many things and be rejected by the elders, chief priests and teachers of the law, and that He must be killed and after three days rise again" **(Mark 8:31).**

Goal

We seek to understand Jesus' revelation of Himself as the Christ, His teaching that the Christ must suffer, and His call for His disciples to be willing to lose their lives for His sake.

What's Going On Here?

As in the previous lesson, we see Jesus teaching His disciples in word and by action, leading them to the confession that He is the Christ. Once they made that confession, He began to teach them that He must suffer, be killed, and rise again from the dead. His disciples are called to follow Him in self-denial and sacrifice. Even the glimpse of His glory revealed in His transfiguration is framed by His teaching that His mission required Him to suffer, die, and rise again.

Searching the Scriptures

Mark seems to have arranged **chapter 8** to parallel **6:31–7:37.** Both start with a miraculous feeding of a multitude, followed by a crossing of the Sea of Galilee, a conflict with the religious leaders, a conversation about bread, a healing, and finally a confession of faith. Perhaps Mark was highlighting the fact that the disciples had to experience these things twice before they understood what the acts and teaching said about Jesus, before they could make a confession about who Jesus is.

The second feeding of a multitude seems to have occurred on the east side of the Sea of Galilee in the region of the Decapolis **(7:31),** a largely Gentile area, although sizeable numbers of Jews lived there as well. Thus those listening to Jesus' teaching were probably a mixed group of Jews and Gentiles.

1. Read **8:1–10.** In the account recorded in **Mark 6,** Jesus had compassion on the crowd because they were like sheep without a shepherd, and so He taught them **(6:34).** What invoked Jesus' compassion this time? Why were the people in this condition?

The disciples' response lacks the tone of disrespect present in the previous account. They could hardly have forgotten Jesus' earlier miracle. Perhaps they did not want to presume that He would repeat it. Or perhaps they were too dull of faith to think He would. However, to repeat it is exactly what Jesus intended.

2. What would Jesus' prayers of thanksgiving have taught the Gentiles in the crowd? (Thanking God for bread was the common way the Jews began a meal.)

3. Read **8:11–13.** The Pharisees intended to test Jesus to see if His ministry was indeed from God. The sign that they ask for was not a miracle. They had witnessed some of Jesus' miracles and perhaps were among those who accused Him of performing miracles with satanic power **(3:22).** They wanted a definitive sign from God that Jesus' ministry was from Him. Why did Jesus refuse to comply?

4. Read **8:14–21.** Yeast, which penetrates the dough with which it is mixed, was a common metaphor for corrupting influences. Fresh from His debate with the Pharisees, Jesus warned His disciples to beware of the disposition of the Pharisees that demanded a sign and the yeast of Herod, lest they too be corrupted. Exactly what Jesus meant by the yeast of Herod is not clear, but we do know that Herod was not a fine example of faith. But the disciples did not understand what Jesus was saying. The mention of yeast reminded them that they had no bread. Why did Jesus rebuke them?

Read **8:22–26** and **Isaiah 35:4–5.** Here again (as in the healing of the deaf and mute man in **Mark 7**), we see Jesus fulfilling the prophecy of what God would do when He came to save His people.

5. Read **8:27–30.** Finally, the blind eyes and the deaf ears of the disciples were opened. What did Peter confess? Why did Jesus warn the disciples not to tell anyone?

6. Read **8:31–33.** Jesus did not use the title *Christ* for Himself, probably because of the false expectations associated with it. But once the disciples recognized that He was the Christ, Jesus began to instruct them about what His mission as the Christ entailed, what God's plan for the Messiah was. What did Jesus teach His disciples that He, the Christ, would have to do? How did Peter show that this was not his idea of what the Christ would do? Where did Jesus say Peter's ideas came from?

7. Read **8:34–9:1.** This concept of a suffering Messiah had implications also for the disciples of the Messiah. What did Jesus teach that all who would be His disciples must do **(8:34)**? What does that mean?

8. For whose sake are disciples to be willing to give their lives **(8:35)**? While this kind of sacrifice doesn't make sense according to the world's standards, what are the ultimate consequences of doing it or seeking not to do it **(8:35–37)**?

9. While stressing the suffering aspect of His mission, Jesus also pointed forward to His glory that would follow. Who will not be allowed to share in that glory **(8:38)**?

10. Note that in **8:31, 38,** Jesus used His favorite self-designation, "the Son of Man." Since this was a common Aramaic expression, the disciples may not have immediately caught its implications. But by using it in contexts like **8:38** while discussing His glory, Jesus showed that He is the Son of Man of **Daniel 7:13–14.** How is the Son of Man pictured there?

The exact meaning of **Mark 9:1** is not clear. Some think that it refers to the transfiguration of Jesus, the account of which immediately follows in **Mark.** There some of the disciples glimpsed Jesus' glory before they tasted death. Other scholars think that this passage refers to the outpouring of the Holy Spirit at Pentecost and the powerful spread of the kingdom that occurred during the lifetime of the apostles as a result of their Spirit-inspired witness.

Read **9:2–8.** The transfiguration of Jesus is rich in Old Testament allusions. It occurred on a mountain as did the great manifestations of God that Moses and Elijah saw on Mount Sinai (Horeb; **Exodus 24; 1 Kings 19**). Jesus appeared with these two great Old Testament prophets, Moses, the symbol of the Old Covenant about to be fulfilled through Jesus, and Elijah, the one who was to appear again before the great and terrible day of the Lord to prepare people for His coming **(Malachi 4:5–6).** The cloud recalled the form in which God appeared to His people in the Old Testament **(Exodus 24:15–16; 40:34–35; 1 Kings 8:10–11).**

11. In words reminiscent of those He spoke at Jesus' Baptism, what did God the Father say about Jesus (see also **Deuteronomy 18:15**)? Why would this glimpse of Jesus' glory and this affirmation of His divine sonship be important for the disciples in days to come?

Read **Mark 9:9–13.** As they were coming down the mountain, Jesus redirected the disciples' attention from their experience of His glory to the suffering that must precede the full disclosure of that glory. The disciples were curious about the prophecy that Elijah must come to restore all things. Jesus said that indeed Elijah had come, a reference to John the Baptist. But that did not mean that the Son of Man did not have to suffer and be rejected. It was to this goal that Jesus' sight was directed.

The Word for Us

1. Lest you judge the disciples too harshly, talk about the temptations you face to put temporal needs above living as a faithful disciple.

2. It is hard for most of us to imagine being in a situation where we would be called on to give up our lives for Jesus and the Gospel, although that day may come for some of us. What other sacrifices might we more regularly be called on to make, sacrifices that require us to deny ourselves?

3. What can give us hope when it seems like evil is about to overwhelm the Gospel and the church?

Closing

Sing or read together the following stanzas of "Oh, Wondrous Type! Oh, Vision Fair":

Oh, wondrous type! Oh, vision fair
Of glory that the Church may share,
Which Christ upon the mountain shows,
Where brighter than the sun He glows!

And faithful hearts are raised on high
By this great vision's mystery,
For which in joyful strains we raise
The voice of prayer, the hymn of praise.

O Father, with th'eternal Son
And Holy Spirit ever one,
We pray You, bring us by Your grace
To see Your glory face to face.

To Do This Week

As noted in the introduction, you will benefit from reading through the entire gospel several times. For next time, pay particular attention to **Mark 9:14–10:45.**

Lesson 6

Discipleship = Servanthood (Mark 9:14–10:45)

Theme Verses

"Whoever wants to be first must be slave of all. For even the Son of Man did not come to be served, but to serve, and to give His life as a ransom for many" (Mark 10:44–45).

Goal

We seek to understand the essence of Jesus' mission—to give His life as a ransom for many—and His call to follow Him in service.

What's Going On Here?

Jesus continued to teach His disciples about the kingdom—a gift that must be received like a child—about the goal of His mission, and about the nature of discipleship. But the import and reality that Jesus must suffer and die didn't yet register with the disciples, who were more concerned about glory and rank within the kingdom. In response to their grasping for glory and greatness, Jesus taught that to follow Him means to follow Him first in service and suffering and only then in glory. As an example to those who would follow Him He held up Himself—the Son of Man whose express purpose in coming was to serve and to give His life to ransom people from sin and death.

Searching the Scriptures

1. Read **9:14–29.** Jesus' words to the disciples in **9:29** indicate that they had not prayed when they were trying to exorcise the demon. Apparently they had forgotten that the power to cast out demons did not reside in

them, but that they were dependent on God for that power. The disciples' inability to heal the boy had shaken the father's faith in Jesus' ability to do so. Jesus called the man back to faith, reminding him that with God all things are possible. How did the man respond **(9:24)?** What important things did the man recognize?

Read **9:30–32.** Jesus focused His attention on teaching His disciples, specifically about what was to happen to Him—that He was going to be delivered up to people who would kill Him but that after three days He would rise again. But the disciples did not understand and were afraid to ask what He meant, perhaps afraid of the pain understanding would bring.

2. Read **9:33–37.** People in first-century Jewish culture were preoccupied with rank. Being men of their culture, the disciples were arguing about which of them was the greatest. What did Jesus say about how one becomes great in the kingdom of God? How does that fit in with Jesus' teaching about discipleship in **8:34** and with His mission? What did Jesus say about welcoming children, an example of those lowest by the world's standards?

3. Read **9:38–42.** Although it is not specifically stated, we can presume that the person rebuked by the disciples was a believer, not just someone using Jesus' name in a magical way (see **Acts 19:13–16**). What did Jesus say about trying to exclude those who would participate in His ministry? To what tasks does participation in His ministry extend? Why should we be careful not to cause even those we might deem least in the kingdom to sin?

4. Read **Mark 9:43–50.** Not only are Jesus' disciples to avoid causing others to sin, they are to remove from their lives anything that would cause them to sin. Jesus taught this to His disciples using exaggerated figures of speech. What contrast did He make? What did He say about hell? **Mark 9:49** may be a reference to the fire of suffering and purification that Jesus' disciples must undergo in this life. What did Jesus caution the disciples to do in **9:50?**

Read **10:1–12.** Jesus had begun His journey to Jerusalem to fulfill His mission. He was tested by the Pharisees with a question about divorce. Jesus may well have been across (on the east side) of the Jordan in Herod's territory, and the Pharisees may have been seeking to get Him into trouble with Herod. Recall that John the Baptist had confronted Herod about his marriage to Herodias.

5. Moses did not actually condone or authorize divorce but attempted to limit its evil consequences (see **Deuteronomy 24:1–4**). According to Jesus, why did he do that? Why is divorce wrong?

6. Read **Mark 10:13–16.** What was Jesus' reaction to the disciples' assumption that children were not important to Him? Adults are often reluctant to have things given to them. They want to earn them or think that they have in some way merited them. Children on the other hand are glad recipients. The kingdom of God is a gift. Why is it necessary to be like children to enter it?

Read **10:17–23.** Following Jesus' teaching that the kingdom is a gift that must be received like a child, Mark recorded an incident about a man who thought he could earn eternal life. Perhaps Jesus asked the man why he called Him good to see if the man really understood that he was talking to God or to encourage him to consider the identity and nature of the one to whom he spoke. The man thought that he had kept the commandments but knew that he did not have eternal life. Jesus saw that there was one obstacle in the man's life that had to be cleared before he could see his inability to merit eternal life and instead receive it from Jesus. That was the man's attachment to his wealth.

Evidently the man had made his wealth an idol, finding security in it rather than in God alone. It is likely that the man thought that his wealth was a sign of God's favor, a popular belief in Jesus' day, based on passages such as **Job 1:10** and **Psalm 128:1–2.** Jesus called the man to turn his back on what he thought was the sign of God's favor and to find God's favor through Jesus.

7. Jesus wasn't calling the man to earn eternal life by giving away all his possessions but calling him to discipleship. How do Jesus' words to the man echo His teaching in **Mark 8:34–36?**

Note that Jesus' instructions to the man to sell all that he had and give it to the poor do not apply to all who would follow Jesus. They were addressed to that particular man and are applicable only to those who are in the same spiritual condition.

8. Read **10:24–27.** Jesus used the incident with the rich man to point out how difficult it is for anyone, but especially the rich, to enter the kingdom of God. The disciples were amazed and asked who then can be saved. What did Jesus' response say about the source of salvation and about human efforts to earn or merit it?

9. Read **10:28–31.** In contrast to the rich young man, Peter pointed out, with a note of pride, that the disciples had left all to follow Jesus. What promise did Jesus make in response?

Read **10:32–34.** This was Jesus' third prophecy of His coming death and resurrection. Note that Jesus knew in detail what was going to happen to Him. Many of these details are spelled out in Old Testament prophecies such as **Psalm 22:6–8** and **Isaiah 50:6.**

Jesus' previous prophecy of His passion was followed by the disciples' argument about who was the greatest and Jesus' teaching about greatness in the kingdom **(Mark 9:31–35).** After this prophecy, too, glory was on the mind of the disciples.

Read **10:35–45.** James and John requested that when Jesus was revealed in glory that He give them the highest places of honor. Jesus asked them whether they could share in His suffering and death. Of course, no one could do that. But showing ignorance, James and John claimed they could. Jesus affirmed that indeed they would be persecuted and suffer for Him and the Gospel, yet it was the Father's prerogative to assign places of honor in the kingdom. Concerned lest James and John gain some advantage over them, the other 10 became indignant. Jesus again taught them that those who would be great in the kingdom must be servants. Jesus held Himself before the disciples as an example.

10. What did He say about His mission?

The Word for Us

1. Whom should the church allow to participate in the work of the kingdom? How can we keep from having an overly narrow view of that work? What dangers should we be wary of?

2. Discuss ways that all believers, but especially those who exercise leadership in the church, can remind themselves that they are servants. How can you live out your servant role?

Closing

Pray this prayer together:

Almighty God, whose Son Jesus Christ chose to suffer pain before going up to joy, and crucifixion before entering into glory, mercifully grant that we, walking in the way of the cross, may find this path to be the way of life and peace; through Jesus Christ, Your Son, our Lord, who lives and reigns with You and the Holy Spirit, one God, now and forever. Amen.

© 1982 CPH.

To Do This Week

As noted in the introduction, you will benefit from reading through the entire gospel several times. For next time, pay particular attention to **Mark 10:46–12:12.**

Lesson 7

The Messiah Enters His Capital (Mark 10:46–12:12)

Theme Verse

"Jesus entered Jerusalem and went to the temple" **(Mark 11:11).**

Goal

We seek to understand why Jesus entered Jerusalem as He did and how He responded to what He found there.

What's Going On Here?

Jerusalem, the capital of the davidic kings. Jerusalem, site of the temple, the center of Israel's life and worship. Jerusalem, a city that should have been characterized by righteousness and justice. Jerusalem, the city that should have welcomed its Messiah with eager expectation.

Humbly, Jesus entered Jerusalem as the Messiah to shouts of praise and to royal treatment by the crowds. But that was as far as His welcome extended. When Jesus went to the temple, He did not find the reverence for God that should have been there. And from the religious leaders He received only questioning and rejection.

Searching the Scriptures

1. Read **10:46–52.** Although Jesus was resolutely heading for Jerusalem, He took time to heal someone who appealed to Him in faith. What connotations did the title *Son of David* have (see **Isaiah 11:1–3**

[Jesse was the father of David]; **Jeremiah 23:5–6; Ezekiel 34:23–24**)?

Read **Mark 11:1–11.** Jerusalem and the road to Jerusalem were crowded with pilgrims going there for the feast of Passover. Recall that Passover was one of the three yearly feasts that people were required to celebrate in Jerusalem. Jesus entered Jerusalem as the Messiah to the praise of the crowd. *Hosanna* is a Hebrew expression that literally means "save us!" It came to be used as an exclamation of praise. "Hosanna! Blessed is He who comes in the name of the Lord!" **(11:9)** is from **Psalm 118:25–26. Psalm 118** is one of the praise psalms used in connection with Passover.

2. Why were the shouts of the people appropriate for Jesus' entry even if their full significance wasn't recognized until later? How was the humility of Jesus shown in this incident? How did Jesus fulfill **Zechariah 9:9?**

Read **11:12–14.** In the Old Testament, the prophets sometimes used symbolic actions to convey their message (for example, **Isaiah 20; Jeremiah 13:1–11; Ezekiel 4**). In a similar way, Jesus may have been acting out a prophecy using a fig tree.

3. What was the condition of the fig tree? What might this have symbolized about Jerusalem (see **Micah 7:1–6**)? In that case what would Jesus' words have meant for Jerusalem?

4. Read **Mark 11:15–19.** The area where commerce was taking place was the Court of the Gentiles. What did the commercial activity prevent people from doing (note that this was the only part of the temple into which Gentiles were allowed)? What was Jesus defending by driving the merchants from the temple? Why did this incident cause the religious leaders to plot Jesus' death?

5. Read **11:20–25.** What are two necessary components of effective prayer? How was Jesus' teaching here balanced by His own example in Gethsemane **(14:36)?** How does unforgiven sin put a barrier between us and God?

6. Read **11:27–33.** The religious leaders questioned Jesus about who had given Him the authority to cleanse the temple. In a tactic common to the debating style of the day, Jesus responded with a question of His own. In His response, Jesus linked His authority with that of John the Baptist. If the religious leaders had acknowledged that John's baptism came from God, what would that have implied about Jesus' authority? Why did they not answer according to what they truly thought?

7. Read **Mark 12:1–12** and **Isaiah 5:1–7.** Jesus began His parable by describing the vineyard exactly as Isaiah had done in his parable, thus bringing Isaiah's parable immediately to the mind of His hearers and implying that the situation was the same then as now. Unlike Jesus' earlier parables, this one was meant to be understood by the unbelieving leaders. Whom did the landlord represent? the tenants? the vineyard? the repeated messengers? the son? What did the landlord rightfully expect?

8. When the tenants saw the son, they assumed that the landlord had died and that if they killed the son then they could claim the land. What consequences were in store for those rebellious tenants? Who are the others to whom the vineyard would be given?

9. Jesus ended by quoting **Psalm 118:22–23** and applying it to Himself. He is the stone the builders rejected but that God has used as the key stone in the building. What was Jesus trying to communicate to the religious leaders? Did they understand the parable? Did they heed the warning?

The Word for Us

1. How can we guard against making the church a commercial or political venture?

2. What does this lesson teach about the consequences of rejecting Jesus? Why is it so important to share the Gospel even in the face of rejection?

Closing

Sing or read together the following stanza of "Hosanna, Loud Hosanna":

"Hosanna in the highest!"
    That ancient song we sing,
For Christ is our Redeemer,
    The Lord of heav'n our King.
Oh, may we ever praise Him
    With heart and life and voice
And in His blissful presence
    Eternally rejoice!

To Do This Week

As noted in the introduction, you will benefit from reading through the entire gospel several times. For next time, pay particular attention to **Mark 12:13–13:37.**

Lesson 8

Jesus' Death Draws Near
(Mark 12:13–13:37)

Theme Verse

[Jesus said,] "What I say to you, I say to everyone: 'Watch!'" (**Mark 13:37**).

Goal

We seek to understand some of Jesus' final teachings before His arrest.

What's Going On Here?

The time for Jesus' death was drawing near. The religious leaders tried several times to trap Him in His words. But He amazed them with His answers. When they were silenced, Jesus challenged them with a question designed to stimulate them to examine their expectations of the Messiah.

Jesus then instructed His disciples about things to come, preparing them for the time when He would be taken from them. He talked to them about the destruction of Jerusalem, about the persecutions they would face, and about His return in glory. His words call all of His disciples to vigilance as they await His return.

Searching the Scriptures

Read **12:13–17.** Jesus' opponents intended the question they asked to put Jesus in a dilemma. If He answered that taxes should be paid to Caesar, He would be discredited with the people who felt that taxes were a humiliating sign of Rome's rule over them. If Jesus said that taxes were not to be paid, His enemies could have accused Him of treason to the Roman authorities.

Part of the reason Roman rule was so distasteful to the Jews was that the emperor claimed to be divine. The abbreviated inscription on the front of the coin that Jesus asked to see was this: "Tiberius Caesar Augustus, Son of the Divine Augustus."

1. By His reply, what was Jesus saying about paying taxes? What was He saying about the supposed divinity of Caesar?

As was common among scholarly debates of the day, the surface question asked by the religious leaders may have also hinted at a deeper question and that is this: "If you are the Messiah, why are we still under Roman rule?" In that case, Jesus' response would have indicated to the religious leaders that they were concerned about the wrong enemy. Their real enemies were sin and death, and by comparison Rome was nothing to worry about. It was these greater enemies that Jesus had come to defeat.

2. What was the reaction of the religious leaders to Jesus' answer?

Read **12:18–27.** This question too was designed to discredit Jesus. The Sadducees did not believe that people would live again after death. Their question was intended to highlight the difficulties that would be encountered if there indeed were a resurrection. Thus, they intended to make belief in the resurrection seem ridiculous, and they hoped to make Jesus look ridiculous trying to defend it. Central to their argument was the Jewish belief that family relationships would be the same in heaven as they are here on earth.

3. According to Jesus, what was the basis of their error? What did Jesus teach about marriage in heaven?

The only part of Scripture that the Sadducees considered valid was the Pentateuch, the first five books of Moses. Note that Jesus' final argument was drawn from this part of Scripture.

4. When the Jews of Jesus' day talked about God as the God of Abraham, Isaac, and Jacob, they were acknowledging that God was the protector and Savior of their forefathers. What did Jesus' reply say about the extent to which God was the patriarchs' protector and Savior?

5. Read **12:28–34.** What did both Jesus and the teacher of the law agree is the central concern of God? What is the basis of our love for God **(12:29)?** Why did Jesus' answer include two commandments when the question only asked for one?

Read **12:35–37.** Jesus Himself took a turn at asking a question. His question revolved around the relationship between the witness of Scripture that the Messiah would be David's son and that He would be David's Lord. The people's hope for a Messiah was based in part on God's promise to David that "your house and your kingdom will endure forever before Me; your throne will be established forever" **(2 Samuel 7:16).** In Jesus' day most Jews expected that the Messiah, in fulfillment of this promise, would set up an earthly kingdom, such as David had. But Jesus taught them that they were missing something important. The Messiah was not only David's descendant, but also David's Lord.

6. In order to fulfill both **2 Samuel 7:16** and **Psalm 110:1,** which Jesus quoted in **Mark 12:36,** where would the Messiah's throne be situated? What did this imply about Jesus' nature? What did it imply about whom Jesus came to do battle with?

7. Read **12:38–40.** What was the heart of Jesus' warning about the teachers of the law?

8. Read **12:41–44.** In contrast to the teachers of the law, what did this woman demonstrate by her gift?

Read **13:1–13.** Jesus used the opportunity afforded by the disciples' question to instruct them about the turbulent times to come, times when He would no longer be physically with them. In a method similar to that used by Old Testament prophets, Jesus referred to things that were to happen shortly and events that will happen at the end of time, all blended into one panoramic picture.

> These verses supply a good illustration of prophetic "foreshortening" of history. ... This foretelling [of prophecy] is done in a "two dimensional" manner, in that the perspective of time is usually either lacking or vague. This may well be because time has no independent existence outside our temporal order. ... This prophetic "foreshortening" often passes over in silence, in the sequence of the several events, the vast stretches of time that separate them, and so joins closely events which are actually far apart.
>
> Here God's immediate judgment on His people at one particular point in history is almost imperceptibly dovetailed into His universal judgment on all humanity at the last day. Since both are manifestations of God's continual ongoing judgment on human sin and rebellion, the whole makes sense (R. Alan Cole, *The Gospel According to Mark: An Introduction and Commentary*, Tyndale New Testament Commentaries, Revised Edition [Grand Rapids, MI: Eerdmans, 1989], pp. 278–79).

9. Jesus' primary purpose in this discourse appears to have been to call His followers to vigilance. What did Jesus instruct His disciples to watch

out for in **13:5–6?** Are wars, earthquakes, and famines signs that the end of the world is imminent?

10. Jesus was clear that His followers would be persecuted because they follow Him. But in spite of persecution, what *must*, according to God's divine plan, happen before the end of the world **(13:10)?** What is the disciples' source of boldness and defense when they are brought before civil authorities for the sake of Jesus **(13:11)?** What is in store for those who stand firm in the faith—in the face of hatred, even from family members—until the end **(13:12–13)?**

Read **13:14–23.** Here Jesus was clearly talking about the destruction of Jerusalem and answering the specific question asked by the disciples. **Mark 13:14** contains a quotation from **Daniel** about a coming desolation that was to be the signal for Jesus' followers to flee immediately. **Luke (20:21)** understood this signal to be armies surrounding Jerusalem. The church in Jerusalem heeded Jesus' warning, fleeing across the Jordan River to the city of Pella shortly before the Romans destroyed Jerusalem in A.D. 70. In **13:19** Jesus described the enormity of the destruction in words similar to those used by the historian Josephus, who witnessed the destruction of the city. Shortly after destroying the city, Rome became preoccupied with affairs back home and hastily withdrew many troops, thus cutting short the destruction, something God caused to happen for the sake of the elect **(13:20).** During those days, many false messiahs arose. But Jesus had forewarned His disciples not to be deceived by them.

Read **13:24–31.** With only a vague reference to the time intervening ("in those days, following that distress"), Jesus then began to teach about His return.

11. What will happen to the elect (all believers in Christ) when the Son of Man comes in the clouds with great power and glory? What assurance did Jesus give His disciples in **13:31?** It is unclear whether **13:28–30** refers to the destruction of Jerusalem or the end of the world.

12. Read **13:32–37.** What attitude toward the end of the world did Jesus instruct His followers to have? Why? What are they to do in the meantime **(13:34)?**

The Word for Us

1. What should be the concern of all Christians while awaiting the return of Christ (see **12:29–31; 13:10**)? While we long for Christ to come, why are we also thankful that He delays His return (see **2 Peter 3:3–9**)?

2. Why should we be wary of those people who are constantly trying to

predict when the end of the world will be? What do you think Jesus meant when He said to be watchful for His return?

Closing

Sing or read together the following stanzas of "Rise, My Soul, to Watch and Pray":

Watch against yourself, my soul,
  Lest with grace you trifle;
Let not self your thoughts control
  Nor God's mercy stifle.
Pride and sin
  Lurk within,
All your hopes to shatter;
  Heed not when they flatter.

But while watching, also pray
  To the Lord unceasing.
God alone can make you free,
  Strength and faith increasing,
So that still
  Mind and will
Heartfelt praises tender
  And true service render.

To Do This Week

As noted in the introduction, you will benefit from reading through the entire gospel several times. For next time, pay particular attention to **Mark 14.**

Lesson 9

Jesus Is Condemned to Die (Mark 14)

Theme Verse

"They all condemned [Jesus] as worthy of death" **(Mark 14:64).**

Goal

We seek to understand the circumstances behind Jesus' condemnation to die and the significance of His death for us.

What's Going On Here?

The final hours of Jesus' mission had arrived. Jesus received an anointing for His burial, instituted the Lord's Supper at His last Passover celebration, and predicted that His followers would desert Him. He pleaded with His Father in prayer that the cup He was about to drink be removed. But when it was evident that His Father wanted His mission to proceed, Jesus willingly submitted to the Father's will and went to meet those sent to arrest Him. In front of His accusers Jesus sat silent until asked point blank whether He was the Messiah. He boldly affirmed that He was (at the same time that Peter was denying association with Him) and was condemned to die for His confession.

Searching the Scriptures

1. Read **14:1–11.** In contrast to the plotting of the religious leaders and Judas to kill Jesus, what did the woman's action show? What did Jesus say that she was doing? How did Jesus' words in **14:9** point beyond His death? Why was Judas' offer to betray Jesus important to the plan of the religious

leaders expressed in **14:1–2?**

Read **14:12–26.** Jesus' last meal before His death was the Passover meal. The Passover was the celebration where God's people recalled His deliverance of their forefathers from Egypt **(Exodus 12).** As they did so the people anticipated the day when God would again intervene to save them. The Passover pointed forward to the Messiah and His sacrifice. By identifying the bread of the Passover meal as His body and the wine as His blood, Jesus was indicating that He was fulfilling the Passover (which after His death had served its purpose) and bringing the salvation for which the people longed.

2. What violated the fellowship of the Passover meal (see also **Psalm 41:9**)? What did Jesus' words about His betrayer say about God's will, about Judas' responsibility for his actions, and about Jesus' ultimate vindication (see also **Psalm 41:10–12**)?

3. Just as the covenant on Sinai was ratified by blood **(Exodus 24:8),** so the new covenant (solemn agreement) that God was making with His people through the death of the Messiah would be ratified with the Messiah's blood. How did Jesus' words in **Mark 14:24** echo **Mark 10:45** and **Isaiah 53:12?** What additional information about this sacrifice do the last two passages give? To what do Jesus' words in **14:25** point forward (see also **Revelation 19:6–9**)?

4. Read **Mark 14:27–31** and **Zechariah 13:7–9.** According to **Zechariah,** of what process were the striking of the shepherd and the scattering of the sheep (the disciples) a part? Again, of what did Jesus assure His disciples in **Mark 14:28?** What was behind Peter's declaration that he would follow Jesus into death before he would disown Him?

5. Read **14:32–42.** The hour was near when the Son of Man would be betrayed into the hands of sinners. The hour was also near when the declarations of Peter **(14:31),** James, and John **(10:38–39)** that they would share His suffering were to be tested. What did Jesus do as the hour approached? Three times He interrupted Himself to encourage the three disciples to do the same. Why **(14:38)?**

6. The cup Jesus was about to drink filled Him with sorrow to the point of death. What was this cup (see **Isaiah 51:17, 22**)? This last verse promises Israel that someone else—Jesus—would drink the cup for them. What did the way Jesus addressed God show about His relationship with Him? How did Jesus' prayer show His obedient submission? How did His words in **Mark 14:42** show the same?

Read **14:43–52.** Jesus' arrest had been ordered by the Sanhedrin, the Jewish ruling council, the components of which are listed in **14:43.** This council had some jurisdiction to deal with civil and criminal matters that did not involve Roman citizens.

Jesus, the sinless Son of God, was humiliatingly arrested like a violent criminal. Jesus pointed out the irony of the party coming to take Him by force when He had been in their midst in the temple. The Scriptures to which Jesus referred in **14:49** likely include **Isaiah 53:12** ("was numbered with the transgressors") and **Zechariah 13:7** (quoted by Jesus in **Mark 14:27**). Just as Jesus had said, all His followers deserted Him.

The young man noted in **14:51–52** may have been John Mark, the writer of this gospel. Tradition indicates that Jesus and His disciples had celebrated the Passover meal earlier that night in John Mark's home. The use of the particular Greek term used by Mark for *young man* indicates one who is especially strong and brave. Mark may have seen in this incident a fulfillment of **Amos 2:16.**

Read **14:53–65.** The members of the Sanhedrin had clearly decided to condemn Jesus to death even before hearing the evidence **(14:55).** But they pretended to be administering justice by adhering to the requirement to have two or more witnesses **(Deuteronomy 19:15),** which they were unable to find despite repeated attempts. In fulfillment of **Isaiah 53:7,** Jesus remained silent and did not answer His accusers.

The high priest then decided to interrogate Jesus Himself. The high priest asked Jesus if He was the Messiah. Since the Jews expected the Messiah to prove who He was, it was inconceivable to these men that Jesus could have been in that humiliating position and been the Messiah.

7. How did Jesus' response answer both the question and the implication behind it (see also **Psalm 110:1** and **Daniel 7:13**)? For what did the Sanhedrin condemn Him? What humiliating treatment did they bestow on Him?

8. Read **Mark 14:66–72.** Mark noted the presence of Peter in the courtyard before recounting Jesus' trial to indicate that Peter's experiences were happening at the same time as Jesus' were. In contrast to Jesus' bold proclamation, what did Peter do when confronted? Why? What awoke Peter to what he was doing? How did he feel?

The Word for Us

1. How can Peter's declaration of **14:31** and his subsequent denial be a warning to us? Why are Jesus' words in **14:38** important for us also? What petitions of the Lord's Prayer are particularly applicable when we are faced with persecution and the temptation to deny our Lord? What assurance and strength does Jesus offer us in the Lord's Supper?

2. If Jesus faced rejection, ridicule, and death, should His followers be surprised when they are called upon to face those things because of their association with Him? Of what examples can you think of Christians facing such things today?

Closing

Sing or read together the following stanzas of "The Death of Jesus Christ, Our Lord":

> The death of Jesus Christ, our Lord,
> We celebrate with one accord;
> It is our comfort in distress,
> Our heart's sweet joy and happiness.
>
> He blotted out with His own blood
> The judgment that against us stood;
> He full atonement for us made,
> And all our debt He fully paid.

That this is now and ever true
He gives an earnest ever new:
In this His holy Supper here
We taste His love so sweet, so near.

His Word proclaims and we believe
That in this Supper we receive
His very body, as He said,
His very blood for sinners shed.

To Do This Week

As noted in the introduction, you will benefit from reading through the entire gospel several times. For next time, pay particular attention to **Mark 15–16.**

Lesson 10

Jesus Is Crucified and Rises from the Dead (Mark 15–16)

Theme Verse

"You are looking for Jesus the Nazarene, who was crucified. He has risen! He is not here. See the place where they laid Him" **(Mark 16:6).**

Goal

We seek to understand the events of Jesus' crucifixion and resurrection and what they mean for us.

What's Going On Here?

The Sanhedrin had condemned Jesus to death. Now they accused Him of treason before Pilate that their intentions for Him might be carried out. Behind all of their machinations God was carrying out His plan for the redemption of all people. We will look at how that plan was brought to victorious completion in Jesus' death and resurrection.

Searching the Scriptures

Read **15:1–15.** The Sanhedrin had sentenced Jesus to death, but they had no authority to carry out that sentence. Therefore, they took Jesus to the Roman prefect Pilate. And since blasphemy was not a capital offense under Roman law, the religious leaders twisted Jesus' claim to be the Messiah into a political claim of kingship. They intended for Pilate to think that Jesus was leading an insurrection against Rome (see **Luke 23:1–2**). How ironic that the religious leaders had condemned Jesus for not being the very thing they now accused Him of before Pilate.

1. When Jesus was asked by Pilate whether He was a king, Jesus answered affirmatively, but yet in a way that indicated that He was not the kind of king He was accused of being. What did Jesus tell Pilate about His kingdom according to **John 18:33–38?**

2. In response to the many things the religious leaders accused Him of, Jesus said not a word in defense. Why? What did Pilate think of his silence? Why?

Pilate could find no basis for the charge against Jesus **(John 18:38),** and he knew that the religious leaders were just using him to carry out their own hidden agenda. But instead of just releasing Jesus, he tried to use a Passover custom to get the crowd that had assembled to agree to Jesus' release. The strategy backfired, and the situation was becoming riotous. Therefore, Pilate had Jesus flogged and sentenced Him to be crucified. Flogging was done with a whip consisting of leather thongs plaited with pieces of bone or lead that ripped the victim's flesh. Flogging was a horrible punishment that often resulted in the death of the prisoner.

3. Read **Mark 15:16–20.** How did the soldiers treat Jesus?

Read **15:21–32.** Usually those condemned to die by crucifixion were forced to carry the cross beam of their cross to the execution site. But Jesus, weakened by the flogging, was unable to carry His all the way. The Roman soldiers then forced Simon, a bystander, to carry it for Him.

Crucifixion is one of the most horrible forms of punishment devised by depraved humanity. The victim was nailed (or sometimes tied) to the cross and left to die of exhaustion and ultimately suffocation. The myrrh that Jesus was offered had narcotic properties that were meant to lessen the pain.

4. Why did Jesus refuse the drug?

5. Not only was Jesus subjected to intense pain but also gross humiliation. From whom did Jesus receive insults? Read **Psalm 22:6–18.** What details of Jesus' suffering were prophesied in this passage? You might, as you have time, read the entire psalm.

Read **Mark 15:33–41.** Darkness was one of the 10 plagues that God used to judge the Egyptians before the exodus **(Exodus 10:21–22)**, and the prophets foretold that darkness would accompany the Day of the Lord, the day of God's judgment against human sin **(Amos 8:9–10; Isaiah 13:9–11; Joel 2:30–31)**. That God was judging human sin in the death of Jesus was signified by the supernatural darkness that covered the land. An eclipse is impossible at the time of a full moon; Passover takes place during a full moon.

6. Jesus' words from the cross were a quotation of **Psalm 22:1** and expressed His experience on the cross. Why was Jesus abandoned by God (see **Isaiah 59:2; 2 Corinthians 5:21; Galatians 3:13**)? How did Jesus' words show that He had not given up His faith in God?

7. When Jesus died, the curtain that separated the Holy Place of the temple from the Most Holy Place (Holy of Holies) was torn completely in two. The Most Holy Place could be entered only by the high priest and only on

the Day of Atonement to make atonement for the sins of the people. What did its tearing signify (see **Hebrews 9:11–14; 10:19–22**)?

8. The crucifixion of Jesus is brought to a climax in **Mark** by the confession of the Gentile centurion who had witnessed Jesus' death. What did he confess?

Read **Mark 15:42–47.** In order to bury an executed criminal, it was necessary to receive permission from the Roman authority. Permission was usually granted to members of the family except in cases where the victim was accused of high treason. That Pilate granted permission to someone unrelated in such a case of a person convicted of high treason was another indication that Pilate considered Jesus to be innocent. That Joseph, a prominent member of the Sanhedrin, dared to ask for such permission highlights his commitment to Jesus. Jesus' burial was witnessed by two of the women who had followed Him from Galilee and who had also witnessed His death.

Read **16:1–8.** The devotion of the women to Jesus was shown by their willingness to anoint a body that had been in the tomb for about 36 hours and that in the climate of Palestine should have already begun to decompose. Their proposed action also indicated that they did not expect a resurrection.

The word translated "young man" in **16:5** can indicate a brave young man or an angel. The revelation that the young man spoke to the women indicates that he was an angel.

9. What did the angel make clear about the identity of the man who had risen? Why was it necessary for the angel to explain what happened to the body?

10. Why was Peter singled out to be told of Jesus' meeting the disciples in Galilee? Why would the message have been comforting to all of the disciples?

11. Why were the women afraid (see **9:6**)?

Reliable early copies of **Mark** end here at **16:8.** While few people dispute that **16:9–20** were not originally part of Mark, some argue that the ordinal ending has been lost. However, William Lane makes a credible case for this being the original ending:

> Fear is the constant reaction to the disclosure of Jesus' transcendent dignity in the Gospel of Mark (cf. Chs. 4:41; 5:15, 33, 36; 6:50; 9:6, 32). In the light of this pervasive pattern, the silence and fear of the women are an indirect Christological affirmation. ...
>
> In point of fact, the present ending of Mark is thoroughly consistent with the motifs of astonishment and fear developed throughout the Gospel. These motifs express the manner in which Mark understands the events of Jesus' life. In verse 8 the evangelist terminates his account of the good news concerning Jesus by sounding the note by which he has characterized all aspects of Jesus' activity, his healings, miracles, teaching, the journey to Jerusalem. Astonishment and fear qualify the events of the life of Jesus. The account of the empty tomb is soul-shaking, and to convey this impression Mark describes in the most meaningful language the utter amazement and overwhelming feeling of the women. With his closing comment he wished to say that "the gospel of Jesus the Messiah" (Ch. 1:1) is an event beyond human comprehension and therefore awesome and frightening. In this case, contrary to general opinion, "for they were afraid" is the phrase most appropriate to the conclusion of the Gospel. The abruptness with which Mark concluded his account corresponds to the preface of the Gospel where the evangelist begins by confronting the reader with the fact of revelation in the person of John and Jesus (Ch. 1:1–13). The ending leaves the reader confronted by the witness of the empty tomb interpreted by the word of revelation. The focus

upon human inadequacy, lack of understanding and weakness throws into bold relief the action of God and its meaning (*The Gospel of Mark*, The New International Commentary on the New Testament [Grand Rapids, MI: Eerdmans, 1974], pp. 591–92).

Early attempts to provide another ending to **Mark** included a short ending and a long ending, recorded in **16:9–20,** and the combination of both. Read **16:9–20.** The information found here can be supported from the rest of the New Testament except the reference to drinking deadly poison **(16:18).**

12. In a statement paralleling the Great Commission found in **Matthew 28:19–20** and echoing Jesus' words in **Mark 13:10,** what were the disciples commanded to do **(16:15)?** What will happen to those who believe this Gospel and are baptized? to those who do not believe it?

The Word for Us

1. Why is Jesus' crucifixion and resurrection central to the church's life and teaching? What things sometimes threaten to overshadow the Gospel?

2. What does Jesus' death and resurrection mean for you personally?

3. In what ways can and/or do you participate in the proclamation of the Gospel to the whole world?

Closing

Sing or read together the following stanzas of "Oh, Love, How Deep" (three stanzas of which were used in lesson 1):

For us by wickedness betrayed,
For us, in crown of thorns arrayed,
He bore the shameful cross and death;
For us He gave His dying breath.

For us He rose from death again;
For us He went on high to reign;
For us He sent His Spirit here
To guide, to strengthen, and to cheer.

All glory to our Lord and God
For love so deep, so high, so broad;
The Trinity whom we adore
Forever and forevermore. Amen.

MARK
The Serving Christ

Leaders Guide

Preparing to Teach Mark

In preparation to teach, consult the introduction to the book of Mark in the Concordia Self-Study Bible, and if possible, read the section on Mark in the *Concordia Self-Study Commentary* (CPH, 1979).

Also read the text in a modern translation. The NIV is referred to in the lesson comments.

In the section "Searching the Scriptures," the leader guides discussion, using the questions given (or others) to help the class discover what the text actually says. This is a major part of teaching, namely, directing the learners to discover for themselves.

Another major portion of each lesson is "The Word for Us." This section helps participants, through discussion, to see the meaning of the text for our times, for our church and world today, and especially for our own lives.

Group Bible Study

Group Bible study means mutual learning from one another under the guidance of a leader or facilitator. The Bible is an inexhaustible resource. No one person can discover all it has to offer. In a class many eyes see many things and can apply them to many life situations. The leader should resist the temptation to "give the answers" and so act as an "authority." This teaching approach stifles participation by individual members and can actually hamper learning. As a general rule, the teacher is not to "give interpretation" but to "develop interpreters." Of course there are times when the leader should and must share insights and information gained by his or her own deeper research. The ideal class is one in which the leader guides class members through the lesson and engages them in meaningful sharing and discussion at all points, leading them to a summary of the lesson at the close. As a general rule, don't explain what the learners can discover by themselves.

Have a chalkboard and chalk or newsprint and marking pen available to emphasize significant points of the lesson. Put your inquiries or the inquiries of participants into questions, problems, or issues. This provokes thought. Keep discussion to the point. List on the chalkboard or newsprint the answers given. Then determine the most vital points made in the discussion. Ask additional questions to fill apparent gaps.

The aim of every Bible study is to help people grow spiritually, not merely in biblical and theological knowledge, but in Christian thinking and living. This means growth in Christian attitudes, insights, and skills for Christian living. The focus of this course must be the church and the world of our day. The guiding question will be this: What does the Lord teach us for life today through the book of Mark?

Pace Your Teaching

Depending on the time you have, you may not want to cover every question in each lesson. This may lead to undue haste and frustration. Be selective. Pace your teaching. Spend no more than five to 10 minutes with "Theme Verse," "Goal," and "What's Going On Here?" Take time to go into the text by topic, but not word by word. Get the sweep of meaning. Occasionally stop to help the class gain understanding of a word or concept. Allow approximately 10 to 15 minutes for "The Word for Us." Allowing approximately five minutes for "Closing" and announcements, you will notice, allows you only approximately 30 minutes for "Searching the Scriptures."

Should your group have more than a one-hour class period, you can take it more leisurely. But do not allow any lesson to drag and become tiresome. Keep it moving. Keep it alive. Keep it meaningful. Eliminate some questions and restrict yourself to those questions most meaningful to the members of the class. If most members study the text at home, they can report their findings, and the time gained can be applied to relating the lesson to life.

Good Preparation

Good preparation by the leader usually affects the pleasure and satisfaction the class will experience.

Suggestions to the Leader for Using the Study Guide

The Lesson Pattern

This set of 10 lessons is based on a significant and timely New Testament book—Mark. The material is designed to aid *Bible study*, that is, to aid a consideration of the written Word of God, with discussion and personal application growing out of the text at hand.

The typical lesson is divided into these sections:
1. Theme Verse
2. Goal
3. What's Going On Here?
4. Searching the Scriptures
5. The Word for Us
6. Closing
7. To Do This Week

"Theme Verse," "Goal," and "What's Going On Here?" give the leader assistance in arousing the interest of the group in the concepts of the chapter. Here the leader stimulates minds. Do not linger too long over the introductory remarks.

"Searching the Scriptures" provides the real spade work necessary for Bible study. Here the class digs, uncovers, and discovers; it gets the facts and observes them. Comment from the leader is needed only to the extent that it helps the group understand the text. The same is true of looking up the indicated parallel passages. The questions in the study guide are intended to help the participants discover the meaning of the text.

Having determined what the text says, the class is ready to apply the message. Having heard, read, marked, and learned the Word of God, proceed to digest it inwardly through discussion, evaluation, and application. This is done, as the study guide suggests, by taking the truths found in Mark and applying them to the world and Christianity, in general, and then to personal Christian life. Class time may not permit discussion of all questions and topics. In preparation the leader may need to select one or two and focus on them. These questions bring God's message to the individual Christian. Close the session by reviewing one important truth from the lesson.

Remember, the Word of God is sacred, but the study guide is not. The guide offers only suggestions. The leader should not hesitate to alter the guidelines or substitute others to meet his or her needs and the needs of the participants. Adapt your teaching plan to your class and your class period. Good teaching directs the learner to discover for himself or herself. For the teacher this means directing the learner, not giving the learner answers. Choose the verses that should be looked up in Scripture. What discussion questions will you ask? At what points? Write them in the margin of your study guide. Involve class members, but give them clear directions. What practical actions might you propose for the week following the lesson? A trip to the slums? Interviewing a poor family? Talking about injustice to a county or city administrator? Which of the items do you consider most important for your class?

How will you best use your teaching period? Do you have 45 minutes? an hour? or an hour and a half? If time is short, what should you cut? Learn to become a wise steward of class time.

Be sure to take time to summarize the lesson, or have a class member do it. Plan brief opening and closing devotions using members of the class. In addition, remember to pray frequently for yourself and your class.

Lesson 1
Jesus Begins His Ministry

Theme Verse
Read aloud the theme verse.

Goal
Invite a volunteer to read aloud the goal for this lesson.

What's Going On Here?
Read and discuss the introductory paragraphs.

Searching the Scriptures
1. After Peter's miraculous escape from prison, he went to the home of John Mark's mother, where many Christians were gathered for prayer. John Mark accompanied Saul (Paul) and Barnabas on the first part of their first missionary journey and served as their helper. At Perga John Mark left Paul and Barnabas to return to Jerusalem, an action that led Paul to doubt his trustworthiness as a traveling companion and helper. When Barnabas wanted to take John Mark along on another trip, Paul did not think it wise. Barnabas and Paul had a sharp disagreement over the matter and split up. John Mark then accompanied Barnabas to Cyprus. The rift between Paul and John Mark (who we learn in **Col. 4:10** was the cousin of Barnabas) was eventually healed. John Mark was with Paul when Paul wrote **Colossians,** and Paul later requested that John Mark be sent to him because John Mark was helpful in Paul's ministry.

2. Peter called Mark his son.

3. **Mark** records the beginning of the Gospel (the Good News) about Jesus Christ, the Son of God. Recall that *Christ* (from the Greek) and *Messiah* (from the Hebrew) mean "Anointed One." The Good News that **Mark** records is about Jesus, the long-awaited Messiah, who is also the Son of God. The life, death, and resurrection of Jesus, which is recounted in **Mark,** is the beginning of the Gospel, which has continued since Jesus' ascension as the Good News is proclaimed in all the world and which will not end until Jesus comes again.

4. Although God was making a new beginning, He was also fulfilling promises He had made many years before to His people. John the Baptist was the fulfiller of the prophecies quoted by Mark. His role was a messenger to prepare the way for the Lord. He carried out that role by preaching

that people needed to repent and by baptizing those who repented. Through that Baptism, God conveyed to them forgiveness for their sins. This prepared the people for the coming of the Messiah to whom John pointed forward with his message that one would come after him who was more powerful and who would baptize with the Holy Spirit.

5. Echoing two Old Testament messianic prophecies, God the Father announced that Jesus was His Son whom He loved and with whom He was well pleased. Jesus was empowered for His mission by the Holy Spirit, who descended on Him visibly in the form of a dove. The Spirit sent Jesus into the desert to be tempted by the devil and thus fight His first battle with the archenemy of all people, the one who led humanity into sin and who would have all people suffer the consequences of their sin, eternal separation from God. As we know from **Matt. 4:1–11,** Jesus won this battle with Satan by not succumbing to his temptations.

6. Jesus' message was that the time had come and the kingdom was near. Those who wanted to participate in that kingdom with joy (rather than to experience its coming as judgment) were called to repent (turn from their sins to God) and believe the Good News that Jesus proclaimed.

7. Peter, Andrew, James, and John immediately left everything—their homes, families, and occupations—to follow Jesus, thus illustrating that all other things in life should be secondary to Jesus. Jesus promised to make them fishers of people. They were called to gather people for the coming kingdom.

8. Jesus taught with authority, without quoting human opinions, and He showed His authority over the demon by making him come out of the possessed man. The demon acknowledged Jesus' authority by calling Him the Holy One of God. The people were amazed at what Jesus taught and did. Note that amazement is not the same as belief.

9. Jesus healed the sick and cast the demons out of those possessed. Peter's mother-in-law showed her gratitude to Jesus by waiting on Him and His disciples, exhibiting the kind of humble service that befits all disciples **(10:43–45).**

10. Jesus found a solitary place to pray. Although Jesus willingly healed those who came to Him, His main goal was to proclaim the message of salvation to all people.

11. The leprous man knelt before Jesus and expressed his belief that Jesus could heal him if He were willing. Filled with compassion, Jesus touched the man (probably not a pleasant task), thus defiling Himself according to the Law **(Lev. 13:45–46; 5:2),** and healed him. Jesus did not want people to follow Him because of the miracles alone. He wanted to teach them about the kingdom of God and about the kind of Messiah He

had come to be—one who saves people from their sins **(Matt. 1:21)**—not a political savior, which many were expecting. As a result of the man's disobedience, Jesus was so mobbed by people when He entered a town that He could not do so openly. This may have hindered His teaching ministry. Instead He stayed in uninhabited regions, and even there people came to Him from everywhere.

The Word for Us

1. Jesus shows us the importance of prayer. Jesus made prayer a priority. As those who have been redeemed by the precious blood of Jesus, God invites us to pray and desires that prayer be a priority in our lives.

2. Answers will vary. Jesus has first place in our lives when we recognize that all that we have and are comes from the Lord's hand and when we seek to serve Him in every area of our lives, relying on His power and guidance to do so.

3. Whenever we are directly involved in spreading the Gospel (for example, witnessing, preaching, or teaching) or whenever we support the spreading of the Gospel (for example, through prayer and/or financial support), we are fishers of people.

4. Disobedience has consequences, many of which we cannot foresee. Discipleship means to trust the Lord and obey Him even when we don't understand why we are commanded to do or not do something. Jesus came to earth to suffer and die for our disobedience. His love and forgiveness motivates us to obey Him as faithful servants.

Closing

Sing or read together "Oh, Love, How Deep" as the closing prayer.

To Do This Week

Urge participants to complete the suggested activity.

Lesson 2

Jesus Receives Acclaim and Opposition

Theme Verse
Read aloud the theme verse.

Goal
Invite a volunteer to read aloud the goal.

What's Going On Here?
Read aloud and discuss briefly the introductory paragraph.

Searching the Scriptures

1. The men's persistent actions gave evidence of their faith that Jesus could and would heal the paralytic. Jesus told the paralytic that His sins were forgiven. At first glance that may seem to be an inappropriate response. However, in the Old Testament sin and forgiveness are sometimes connected with disease and healing (see for example **Psalm 103:1–3**). Sickness and death are consequences of sin, although there is usually not a one-to-one correspondence between a particular sin and a particular disease. Nothing in the text indicates that the man was paralyzed because of his particular sins. But like all of us he lived in a world severely warped by sin. Jesus knew that the man would not be whole until his relationship with God, which had been broken by sin, had been restored. Since Jesus would not have announced forgiveness to someone who refused to acknowledge his sin (like many teachers of the law), it seems that Jesus looked into the man's heart and knew that he was bothered by his sin. The man's greatest need was for forgiveness, and Jesus met that need.

2. They were right in thinking that only God or those to whom God has given the authority and power can forgive sins. But they were wrong in refusing to see that God had given this authority to Jesus, and they totally ignored the mounting evidence that in their midst was God in the flesh.

3. Those teachers of the law who were Pharisees objected to Jesus eating (which was a sign of friendship and fellowship) with those whom they considered to be sinners. By sinners, they meant those who did not try to keep the requirements of the Law strictly like they did. Tax collectors especially were outcasts, viewed as lackeys of the hated government. Pharisees thought that contact with those whom they considered to be sin-

ners might defile them, and so they avoided such contact. Jesus pointed out to them that His mission was to call sinners to the kingdom of God. The "righteous," those who did not recognize their sin, did not see their need for Jesus and the salvation He brought.

4. Jesus was saying that just as it was unthinkable to fast at a joyous occasion such as a wedding, so it was unthinkable for His followers to fast while He was present with them because that fact filled them with joy. Pointing forward to the time when He would be taken from them, Jesus said that then it would be appropriate for His followers to fast. Jesus' coming brought about a totally new situation that called for totally new responses, just like new wine had to be poured into new wineskins, not old ones.

5. Correct observance of the Sabbath was of immense importance to the Pharisees. Jesus corrected the Pharisees' narrow, legalistic understanding of the Sabbath by pointing to an incident recorded in the Old Testament **(1 Sam. 21:1–6)** where David had done something that was forbidden when he was in need and was not condemned. Jesus also pointed out that the Sabbath was established by God for the benefit of people (for them to rest and worship), not as an end in itself, which is what the Pharisees had turned it into. Jesus proclaimed that He was the Lord of the Sabbath, thus implying that He had the authority to state how it was to be correctly observed.

6. The answer of course is that it is lawful to do good rather than evil on the Sabbath. The Pharisees did not answer because they refused to acknowledge that their rigid way of observing the Sabbath (which precluded mercy) was displeasing God rather than pleasing Him. Their stubborn hearts made Jesus angry and deeply distressed. The Pharisees further displayed their stubborn hearts by plotting how to kill Jesus. They saw Him as a threat to their whole religious structure. That there were concerns also about Jesus' effect on the political structure is shown by the reference to the Herodians who were supporters of the rule of the Herods.

7. The 12 apostles were to have the special experience of being with Jesus in an intimate way. Answers may vary. That experience fostered learning from Him informally as well as formally, privately as well as in a crowd. It placed the apostles in a position to observe and learn things to which they could later bear witness. These 12 would be sent out by Jesus to preach and would be given authority to cast out demons as His personal representatives; they were to herald the establishment of God's kingdom. Jesus would extend His ministry through them, eventually in ways that were only hinted at this point.

8. In **3:23–26,** Jesus made the point that if Satan were foolish enough to oppose himself, he could not prevail. In **3:27,** Jesus was referring to His battle with Satan. Jesus was the one who was tying up the strong man (Satan) so that He could rob his house.

9. By attributing to Satan Jesus' power to cast out demons which came from the Holy Spirit, the teachers of the law were committing or in danger of committing blasphemy against the Holy Spirit. "In this historical context, blasphemy against the Holy Spirit denotes the conscious and deliberate rejection of the saving power and grace of God released through Jesus' word and act" (William L. Lane, *The Gospel of Mark*, The New International Commentary on the New Testament [Grand Rapids, MI: Eerdmans, 1974], p. 145). By definition, this sin is unforgivable because those who commit it consciously turn their backs on God's salvation, on the only means of receiving His forgiveness. Those who worry about having committed this sin could not have done so since it consists of conscious, deliberate rejection.

10. Those who do God's will are Jesus' brother, sister, and mother.

The Word for Us

1. Answers will vary. Whenever we extend God's grace to people through word or deed, especially to those whom the world considers outcasts, we exhibit the radical nature of the forgiveness and fellowship with God that Jesus brings to all who trust Him as the one who makes that fellowship possible.

2. The Lord instructs us in discipleship through His written Word, the Bible. We learn what the Bible teaches through various means such as personal study, Bible classes, sermons, Christian books, music, and conversations with other Christians. The Holy Spirit works through God's Word to strengthen believer's faith.

Closing

Sing or speak together the selected stanzas of "My Song Is Love Unknown."

To Do This Week

Urge participants to complete the suggested activity.

Lesson 3
The Secret of the Kingdom

Theme Verse
Read aloud the theme verse.

Goal
Read aloud or invite a volunteer to read aloud the goal.

What's Going On Here?
Invite a volunteer to read aloud the introductory paragraph.

Searching the Scriptures
1. Jesus exhorted the people to listen to what He was teaching. For this it is necessary to have ears that are willing to hear, that is, an attitude that wants to learn. Jesus wanted His hearers to listen attentively, seeking to understand what He was teaching them, then believe it and act on it.

2. The secret of the kingdom of God is that in Jesus the promised rule of God has begun. That was contrary to the expectations of many people of Jesus' day about the kingdom. Many expected a kingdom that would be manifested in all its glory immediately, a kingdom whose dawning would bring immediate judgment of God's enemies and vindication of God's people. The secret has been revealed to those who respond to Jesus in faith. The secret is hidden from those who respond with unbelief.

> The citation of Isa. 6:9f. does not mean that "those outside" are denied the possibility of belief. It indicates that they are excluded from the opportunity of being further instructed in the secret of the Kingdom so long as unbelief continues. That the Kingdom has come in an initial phase in the presence of Jesus can be discerned only through faith, which is to say by the grace of God. Jesus' presence, therefore, means disclosure *and* veiling; it releases both grace *and* judgment" (William L. Lane, *The Gospel of Mark*, The New International Commentary on the New Testament [Grand Rapids, MI: Eerdmans, 1974], p. 159).

3. The word that the farmer sows is the message that Jesus has come to bring—that in Him the kingdom of God has begun; in other words, the word is the Gospel. Review **Mark 1:15.** Things that hinder the Gospel from taking root and producing fruit in people's lives are Satan, hardness of heart, shallowness of heart that cannot endure persecution or trouble on account of the Gospel, worries about this life, the deceitfulness of

wealth, and the desire for other things. The seed that falls on fertile soil illustrates those who hear the Gospel, believe it, and produce fruit—whether it be 30, 60, or 100 times what was sown.

4. The more we appropriate the Word sown by Jesus in our lives, the more we will be blessed by it. Those who neglect the Word eventually lose what little understanding of it they did have and thus derive no benefit from it.

5. During this intervening period, the seed grows, resulting in a harvest. The power that produces this growth is in the seed, the Gospel. The sower sows the seed (proclaims the Gospel), then watches it grow, not fully understanding how it does so, and finally harvests the grain.

6. The comparison is made between the smallest of the seeds and the large plant that comes from it, the largest of the garden plants. The kingdom of God, though its beginning in the ministry of the despised and rejected Jesus seems insignificant, will grow into something far beyond human imagination.

7. Jesus stilled the storm with His word. He rebuked the disciples because in spite of their special position of being with Him and having the secret of the kingdom revealed to them, they still did not completely understand who He was or have enough faith in His power not to be afraid. The stilling of the storm revealed that Jesus is both God the Lord and the Savior of His people. What is true about the God who parted the Red Sea—that He is in control of nature and uses His power for the salvation of His people—is also true of Jesus.

8. The demons acknowledged Jesus' superior power by addressing Him as the Son of the Most High God and begged Him not to torment them. The demons were bent on destruction as was shown by the pathetic condition of the man and the killing of the swine.

9. While in fear the people of the region begged Jesus to leave them, the man begged to go with Jesus as a disciple. Jesus instructed the man to return to his home and tell his family how much the Lord had done for him and how He had mercy on him. The man spread the word of what Jesus had done for Him throughout the region of the Decapolis.

10. Jesus' words to her clarified for her that she was healed not merely because she touched His clothes, but through her *faith*. Jesus assured her that her healing was permanent.

11. Jesus called Jairus to have faith that Jesus' power was adequate even for that situation. Jesus showed Himself to be the conqueror also over death. Only the girl's parents and Peter, John, and James were allowed to witness Jesus raising the girl from the dead. Those who ridiculed Jesus were specifically put out of the house before He raised the

girl, again showing that the secret of the kingdom was revealed only to those who had faith.

The Word for Us

1. We should beware of those things that Jesus listed as obstacles to the growth of the Gospel and pray that the Lord would protect us from Satan, keep our faith strong in times of persecution and trouble, enable us to resist the temptations of this life, and make us fruitful soil.

2. As disciples of Jesus we are responsible for sowing the seed (proclaiming the Gospel), but not for making it grow. As the parable of the growing seed and **Rom. 1:16** tell us, the Gospel is the power of God for the salvation of all who believe. It is God who produces growth (faith and fruitfulness) through His Gospel.

3. Responses will vary. Because Jesus is always present with us **(Matt. 28:20),** we need not fear anything that the world or Satan can throw against us.

4. Responses will vary.

Closing

Speak or sing together the stanza of "I Know My Faith Is Founded" printed in the study guide.

To Do This Week

Urge participants to complete the suggested activity.

Lesson 4

A Prophet Is Often without Honor

Theme Verse

Read aloud the theme verse.

Goal

Invite a volunteer to read aloud the goal.

What's Going On Here?

Read aloud and discuss the introductory paragraph.

Searching the Scriptures

1. The people of Jesus' hometown could not see past their familiarity with Him to recognize that His authority and power were from God. The rhetorical questions recorded in **6:3** are derogatory. The people scorned Jesus as a common laborer and as a member of a family whose members they all knew well. The usual custom for referring to a man was to call him the son of his father; for example, Peter was sometimes called Simon bar (son of) Jonah **(Matt. 16:17).** To call someone the son of his mother was an insult. The unbelief of the people kept Jesus from doing many miracles among them.

2. Jesus extended His ministry through the Twelve by giving them the authority and power to act on His behalf. They were to herald the coming of the kingdom by preaching repentance and by healing and casting out demons just as Jesus had been doing. The disciples were forced to depend on God and those whom God would move to provide for them. After leaving a Gentile area, pious Jews would remove the dust from their clothes and sandals to symbolize that they had no part in that place and the coming judgment of it. In a similar gesture, the disciples were to shake the dust of a rejecting town from their feet, thus symbolizing that they had fulfilled their commission and that the people would be judged for their rejection.

3. Some people speculated that Jesus was Elijah, whose coming according to the Old Testament prophet Malachi **(4:5)** was to precede the day when God would come in judgment and salvation. Others said that Jesus was another prophet like the prophets of the Old Testament. A third group of people, including Herod, were obviously unfamiliar with Jesus until after the death of John. This group thought that Jesus was John the Baptist returned from the dead. Herod's belief that Jesus was John raised from the dead would have been particularly disturbing since Herod unjustly had John killed and may have thought that John had come back to haunt him. John was killed because his call to repentance offended Herodias who was able to contrive to have him killed and thus silenced.

4. Jesus had compassion on the people because they were like sheep without a shepherd, without anyone to lead them, guide them, and take care of them. This prompted Jesus to teach them. The disciples showed that they did not fully understand who Jesus was by their disrespectful answer to His command that they feed the multitude (they didn't think to look to Him for help). The inventory of available supplies showed that the situation was beyond human resourcefulness. In both accounts God (in **Exodus,** God the Father; here, God the Son) miraculously fed His people in the wilderness. There is also in each account complaining that shows a lack of faith. In the **Exodus** account the people complained. Here the disciples complained.

5. The disciples' hearts were hardened by unbelief, and thus they did not yet understand that here in their midst was God Himself. Jesus' words echoed the words of God in the Old Testament that His people need not be afraid because He is with them. By walking on the sea, Jesus was doing something that the Old Testament pictured God as doing. Thus Jesus' words and act of walking on the water indicate that He is God. Also, by saying "It is I" **(6:50),** Jesus may have been echoing God's revelation to Moses of His name when He said, "I AM WHO I AM" **(Ex. 3:14).**

6. God is concerned about the uncleanness of people's hearts, not their hands, because that is what makes them sinful rather than holy and prevents them from having fellowship with Him. The obedience that pleases God is also from the heart. Such obedience follows His commands rather than traditions made by people.

7. This woman exhibited faith as shown by her request, her posture when she made the request, her address of Jesus as Lord, and her witty reply. Jesus initially responded in a way designed to test her faith, confirming that she really believed He could heal her daughter. After she confirmed her faith, He responded by casting the demon out of her daughter.

8. The people confessed that Jesus did everything well, that He could make the deaf hear and the mute speak.

The Word for Us

1. The account of the death of John the Baptist would have reassured those facing persecution that their suffering on behalf of the Gospel was not unusual. It tells us that the cost of faithfully following the Lord is sometimes intense persecution and even physical death, and we should not be surprised if someday we are called on to pay that price.

2. Complete wholeness of mind, body, and spirit will be a reality for us in heaven.

Closing

Sing or speak together the hymn stanza printed in the study guide.

To Do This Week

Urge participants to complete the suggested activity prior to the next time you meet.

Lesson 5
The Christ Must Suffer

Theme Verse
Read aloud the theme verse.

Goal
Read aloud or invite a volunteer to read aloud the goal.

What's Going On Here?
Read aloud and discuss the introductory paragraph.

Searching the Scriptures

1. Jesus had compassion on the people because they had been without food for some time and had a long distance to travel before they reached home. They were hungry because they had chosen to be nourished by His teaching for three days and evidently had not brought enough food for that long of a retreat.

2. Jesus' prayers of thanksgiving would have taught the Gentiles to give thanks to God for their daily bread.

3. Jesus did not comply with the Pharisee's request because it stemmed from unbelief. The acts and teachings of Jesus were clear indications of the source of His ministry for those who had the faith to see that. To people of faith a sign was unnecessary, and no sign would have satisfied those who refused to believe.

4. Jesus rebuked the disciples because even after the two miraculous feedings they still did not understand that when they were with Jesus, they need not worry about bread. Here in their midst was God, the source of all food. Rather than focusing on their temporal needs, they should have been trying to understand what He was teaching and to apply it to themselves.

5. Peter confessed that Jesus is the Christ, the Messiah. Recall that *Christ* (from the Greek) and *Messiah* (from the Hebrew) mean "Anointed One." In the Old Testament, prophets, priests, and kings were anointed with oil to consecrate them to the Lord's service. The term *Anointed One* had come to designate the one whom God had promised to send from the line of David to faithfully shepherd His people. Peter confessed that Jesus was that long-expected Christ. But Jesus knew that popular expectations of the Christ were heavily political and nationalistic. Because that was not the kind of Messiah He had come to be, He did not want the disciples to

tell anyone that He was the Christ. Jesus also knew that since He was not what and who the Jewish leaders expected, the proclamation "He is the Christ" would move Him more quickly to death before His work on earth was complete.

6. Jesus taught that He *must* suffer many things, be rejected by the religious leaders, be killed, and after three days rise again. Peter showed that this didn't fit with his expectations of the Messiah by rebuking Jesus. Jesus indicated that Peter's ideas came from Satan, who sought to keep Jesus from His mission.

7. Jesus taught that all who would be His disciples must deny themselves, take up their cross, and follow Him. To deny oneself means to cease to be devoted to oneself, to remove oneself from the center of one's life. A common practice in Jesus' day was that those who were condemned to die by crucifixion had to carry the crossbar of their cross to the execution site. By using this figure of speech Jesus was saying that His disciples must be willing to suffer and die for His sake. Jesus called His disciples to follow Him on a path of self-denial and cross-bearing. Like Jesus, His disciples were to do the will of God, even if that meant sacrificing everything, including their lives.

8. Disciples are to be willing to give their lives for the sake of Jesus and the Gospel. Those who do so will save their lives, that is their spiritual, eternal lives (their souls). Those who seek to save their earthly lives will lose their spiritual, eternal lives.

9. Those who were ashamed of Jesus and His words in this life preferring instead the things of this world will not share Jesus' glory. Instead, Jesus will be ashamed of them.

10. The Son of Man in **Daniel** is a heavenly figure, yet distinct from God the Father, the Ancient of Days. The Son of Man is given sovereign power and glory and authority. That He too is God is shown by the fact that He is worshiped. He is worshiped by people of all nations. His is an everlasting kingdom.

11. God the Father said that Jesus was His Son, whom He loved. He also commanded the disciples to listen to Jesus. This command alluded to the prophecy of a prophet like Moses who was to come and to whom the people were to listen **(Deut. 18:15),** thus showing that Jesus is the fulfillment of that prophecy. This experience would be important to the disciples in days to come when Jesus was to suffer and die because it would affirm that, in spite of His apparent abandonment by God, Jesus was doing God's will and had His full support and approval.

The Word for Us

1. Responses will vary. After participants have shared, assure them of the forgiveness Jesus won for them and all repentant sinners when He died on the cross.

2. Answers will vary. Examples include sacrifices of time, money, honor according to the world's standards, advancement, family ties, friendships.

3. Jesus' transfiguration, resurrection, and promises to return in glory give us the perspective to see that He has won the ultimate victory with His death and resurrection. Though darkness seems to overwhelm the light, it can do so only temporarily.

Closing

Sing or speak together the stanzas of "Oh, Wondrous Type! Oh, Vision Fair" printed in the study guide.

To Do This Week

Urge participants to complete the suggested activity.

Lesson 6

Discipleship = Servanthood

Theme Verse

Read aloud the theme verse.

Goal

Invite a volunteer to read aloud the goal.

What's Going On Here?

Read aloud and discuss the introductory paragraph.

Searching the Scriptures

1. The man confessed his faith but pleaded with Jesus to help his unbelief. The man recognized that his faith was not perfect and that Jesus had the power to strengthen his faith.

2. Jesus said that those who would be great in the kingdom must put others before themselves and be servants of all. This requires the self-

denial that characterizes discipleship. Those who do this follow Jesus who walked the path to glory through servanthood, self-denial, suffering, and sacrifice. Jesus said that those who welcome even the lowest by the world's standards in His name welcome Him and the Father who sent Him.

3. Jesus said that people are either for Him or against Him; they can't be both, and there is no middle ground. Therefore, His disciples ought not to exclude those who wish to do the work of the kingdom. Doing the work of the kingdom extends even to menial tasks, such as giving a representative of Jesus a glass of water because that person is a disciple. Jesus warned that God will punish those who cause a believer to sin, thus we should be careful lest we do that.

4. Jesus made the contrast between removing whatever causes us to sin and entering eternal life with God minus that thing (which is the best for us) and not removing that thing and going to hell still possessing it. Jesus said that the fires of hell never go out. Jesus cautioned His disciples to retain their salt, that which makes them distinctive in the world, that is, faithfulness to Him and the Gospel. And He cautioned them to be at peace with one another, rather than arguing over who is the greatest.

5. Moses provided for the consequences of divorce because of the hardness of the people's hearts, that is their sinful unwillingness to live the way God intended. Divorce is wrong because it violates God's intention and breaks a bond that He has made, something people have no right to do.

Jesus' final pronouncement [10:9] grounds the sanctity of marriage in the authority of God himself. This is consistent with the biblical perspective, which never considers husband and wife alone but always in the presence of God, subject to his commands and aided by his grace. God intended that the purpose of marriage should be unity and that the obligations of marriage should be taken seriously. The decisive "No" to divorce provides the required safeguard against human selfishness which always threatens to destroy marriage. It also warns that the man who dissolves a union sanctioned by God inevitably stands under divine judgment. This warning has in view the husband, rather than a judicial authority, since in Jewish practice divorce was effected by the husband himself. Behind this solemn prohibition there is a deep concern for personal relationships. Jesus does not envisage marriage as it is at times but as it can and should be—a call to fidelity, peace and love. The conclusion of the public discussion shows that this has not been a rabbinic discussion concerning the interpretation of the Law, but an authoritative teaching, astonishingly different from that of the scribes (cf. [Mark] 1:22). The prophetic character of the teaching implies a veiled, messianic proclamation of the Kingdom drawn near in the person of Jesus himself. The disciples are shown that even the ordinances of the Law are not to be followed blindly but are to be carefully considered in the light of the highest standards which Scripture exempli-fies (William L. Lane, *The Gospel of Mark*, The New International Commentary on the New Testament [Grand Rapids, MI: Eerdmans, 1974], pp. 356–57).

6. Jesus was indignant at the disciples' assumption. Only those who know that they are helpless with respect to the kingdom of God and could never earn their way into it will enter it. Like children, they must be willing to be given the kingdom as a gift.

7. Jesus was calling the man to deny himself by giving up his possessions and to follow Jesus. For what would it profit the man to have all the possessions in the world and lose his soul?

8. God alone works salvation; it is impossible for people to earn or merit it.

9. Jesus promised that whatever His followers sacrifice for Him and the gospel will be restored many times over in this life and that in the age to come they will receive eternal life. The reference to family is to the fellowship of other believers, those who are joined in a family based on their obedience to the will of God (see **3:35**). But this earthly life will always be a mixture of blessing and suffering, as Jesus' reference to persecution shows.

10. Jesus taught the disciples that the reason for His coming was to serve and to give His life to ransom many. In Hebrew usage, which was behind the usage here, *many* is an inclusive word that virtually means "all." To ransom means "to pay the price necessary to secure someone's release from bondage." Jesus died to ransom us from bondage to sin and death.

The Word for Us

1. The church should welcome the participation of all who trust in Jesus as Lord and Savior. Answers will vary. We can keep a proper perspective by reminding ourselves that Jesus is the Lord of the church, the one who directs its work, and by trying to see the advantages of having diverse people and churches and organizations doing different things in the kingdom. We should be wary of those who would misrepresent the Gospel or seek to use it to their own advantage.

2. Answers will vary.

Closing

Pray together the Collect for Monday in Holy Week printed in the study guide.

To Do This Week

Urge participants to complete the suggested activity prior to the next time you meet.

Lesson 7

The Messiah Enters His Capital

Theme Verse

Read aloud the theme verse.

Goal

Read aloud or invite a volunteer to read aloud the goal.

What's Going On Here?

Read aloud and discuss the introductory paragraphs.

Searching the Scriptures

1. The Shepherd-King whom God promised to send His people was to be a descendant of David. *Son of David* was a title for the awaited Messiah.

2. The shouts were appropriate because Jesus did come in the name of the Lord to bring the kingdom of David, although that kingdom was not an earthly kingdom like most of the people were expecting. Jesus did come to save His people. He was Jerusalem's King and was worthy of the crowd's praise and royal treatment (the laying of cloaks on the road). Even though Jesus, the Lord of heaven and earth, was entering Jerusalem as its King, He did so on a borrowed colt, without the earthly trappings of wealth and pomp, thus showing His humility. In fulfillment of **Zech. 9:9,** Jesus, Jerusalem's king, came to her, "righteous and having salvation, gentle and riding on a donkey." This caused the people to rejoice and shout as urged in **Zech. 9:9.**

3. The fig tree had leaves but no fruit. This might have symbolized that the worship that took place in Jerusalem was mostly show and did not result in the fruit of faith that God desired. Jesus' words can then be seen as a prophecy of the impending destruction of Jerusalem and its temple (which was carried out by the Romans in A.D. 70). That references to this fig tree were placed by Mark around the account of Jesus' cleansing the

temple lends credence to this interpretation. However, as we will see, the only explicit lesson Jesus drew from the incident concerns a believer's prayer.

4. The commercial activity was preventing prayer. Jesus was defending God's honor and the purpose God had intended for the temple, that it be a house of prayer for *all nations*, as the quotation from Isaiah notes. The religious leaders feared Jesus and His effect on the people.

5. Faith that God can accomplish *anything* and forgiveness are two components of effective prayer. It makes no sense to approach God in prayer if you doubt that He can do what you ask. Another question of course is this: I believe God can do what I ask, but will He? Here Jesus' teaching was balanced by His example in Gethsemane. Like Jesus, believers desire God's will and know that it is best. Thus they include the petition *Your will be done, not mine* in their prayers. When we fail to forgive, there is an unresolved sin between us and God that we need to confess to God and seek His forgiveness and help in overcoming. God's forgiveness of us motivates us to forgive others because we know that their debt to us is a pittance compared to what God has forgiven us (see **Matt. 18:21–35**).

6. Jesus' question was framed to have only two possible answers, either John's baptism was from God or it was not. By bringing John into the discussion, Jesus was implying that however they answered the question would also apply to Him. If the leaders had acknowledged that John's baptism was from God, they would not only have condemned themselves for unbelief, but they would have implied that Jesus' authority also came from God. They were afraid to say that they thought the authority of both John and Jesus was not from God because that view contradicted what the people thought and they were afraid of the people's reaction.

7. The landlord represented God, the tenants the religious leaders, the vineyard the people of God, the repeated messengers the many prophets God had sent His people, and the son Jesus. The landlord expected respect and His share of the crop. If the religious leaders had been faithfully tending the people of God, God would have received the fruits of His people's faith and they would have recognized and welcomed the Messiah rather than killing Him.

8. The tenants would be killed and the vineyard given to others. The others are the new people of God, the church, those who have faith in Jesus as the One sent by God to save the world from sin.

9. Jesus was trying to communicate that if the leaders rejected Him, they would be opposing God Himself and would reap dire consequences. The leaders understood the parable but did not heed the warning, as is shown by their plotting to arrest Jesus.

The Word for Us

1. Answers will vary. We can guard against these things by remembering that the main functions of the church are to spread the Gospel and nurture people in the faith. All other functions are secondary, but we must continually be on guard by the power of the Holy Spirit working through God's Word and constantly be in prayer lest commercial and political ventures overshadow the church's main tasks.

2. Those who reject Jesus oppose God and will face His judgment as did the religious leaders of Jesus' day. The Holy Spirit works through the Gospel to bring people to faith.

Closing

Sing or speak together the stanza of "Hosanna, Loud Hosanna" printed in the study guide.

To Do This Week

Urge participants to complete the suggested activity.

Lesson 8

Jesus' Death Draws Near

Theme Verse

Read aloud the theme verse.

Goal

Invite a volunteer to read aloud the goal.

What's Going On Here?

Read aloud and discuss the introductory paragraphs.

Searching the Scriptures

1. Jesus was saying that taxes are the legitimate domain of the government and as such should be paid. But He was also affirming that Caesar had no right to the claim of divinity. God alone is divine, and He alone should be honored as such.

2. Those who had come to trap Jesus were amazed by His response.

3. Jesus accused the Sadducees of not knowing the Scriptures and of not believing in God's power to raise the dead. That was the basis of their error. Note Jesus' authority in teaching about what life will be like in heaven: People will not live in marriage relationships; they will be like angels, who live in communion with God.

4. Jesus' reply declared that God protected and saved the patriarchs from their greatest enemy—death.

5. Jesus and the teacher of the law agreed that God is most concerned about our wholehearted devotion to Him and that that is lived out in love to our neighbor. "Hear, O Israel: The LORD our God, the LORD is one" **(Deut. 6:4)** indicates

> that the command to love God is an obligation which stems from his uniqueness as God and his gracious favor in extending his covenant love to Israel. It is *the Lord our God* who is to be loved with a completeness of devotion which is defined by the repeated "all." Because the whole man is the object of God's covenant love, the whole man is claimed by God for himself. To love God in the way defined by the great commandment is to seek God for his own sake, to have pleasure in him and to strive impulsively after him. ... The love which determines the whole disposition of one's life and places one's whole personality in the service of God reflects a commitment to God which springs from divine sonship" (William L. Lane, *The Gospel of Mark*, The New International Commentary on the New Testament [Grand Rapids, MI: Eerdmans, 1974], pp. 432–33).

Jesus included the second commandment because the two are inseparable. Those who love God with their whole being will also love their neighbor.

6. The Messiah's throne would be located at the right hand of God. This implied that Jesus is both God and man and that He came not to battle the Romans, but to battle His people's greater enemies—sin, death, and the devil.

7. The heart of Jesus' warning about the teachers of the law was that they were hypocrites. They didn't love God with their whole being and their neighbors as themselves (which is of central concern to God). They cared only about being seen as important in the eyes of people. But, as Jesus warned, they would be severely punished.

8. This woman showed her wholehearted devotion to God and her absolute trust in Him by putting into the treasury all that she had to live on.

9. Jesus instructed His followers to watch out for false teachers, supposedly coming in His name and claiming to be the Messiah, lest the disciples be deceived. Wars, earthquakes, and famines are only the beginning of the suffering that will precede the end of the world.

10. The Gospel must be preached to all nations before the end of the world. The disciples' source of boldness and defense is the Holy Spirit. Those who stand firm will be saved.

11. The elect will be gathered from all over the world by the angels. Jesus assured His disciples that even though heaven and earth would pass away, His words will never pass away.

12. Jesus instructed His followers to always be expecting the end of the world, since it can come any time. No one except the Father knows when that time will be. They are to go about their assigned tasks while being watchful.

The Word for Us

1. While awaiting the return of Christ, His disciples should be totally devoted to God and their neighbors and should be involved in spreading the life-saving Gospel, thankful that while He delays, many yet have the chance to come to repentance and faith.

2. Jesus specifically said that no one knows when the end of the world will be, so it is fruitless to try to figure it out. How can someone figure out something unknown even to Jesus? Answers may vary. During Jesus' earthly ministry He emptied Himself and took on the form of a slave (**Phil. 2:7–8**). He did not always use His divine power, such as omniscience, except when His divine power was needed to accomplish His mission. By calling His disciples to be vigilant, Jesus was telling them not to become complacent and let Him catch them unprepared to meet Him should He return in their lifetime.

Closing

Sing or speak together the stanzas of "Rise, My Soul, to Watch and Pray" printed in the study guide.

To Do This Week

Urge participants to complete the suggested activity.

Lesson 9
Jesus Is Condemned to Die

Theme Verse
Read aloud the theme verse.

Goal
Read aloud or invite a volunteer to read aloud the goal.

What's Going On Here?
Read aloud and discuss briefly the introductory paragraph.

Searching the Scriptures

1. The woman expressed love for, faith in, and thanksgiving to Jesus by anointing Him with expensive perfume. Jesus said that she was anointing His body in preparation for burial. Jesus pointed beyond His death by saying that the Gospel would be proclaimed throughout the world. The religious leaders wanted to arrest Jesus quietly so as not to provoke a riot. Judas' assistance would make it easier to do that.

2. The presence of one who would betray Jesus violated the fellowship of the Passover meal. Jesus said that all that was to happen to Him was in fulfillment of Scripture, thus showing that it was in conformity with the will of God. But Judas would still be held responsible for his traitorous betrayal. Jesus' words of woe to Judas pointed forward to Jesus' ultimate vindication by God.

3. All of these passages stress that the Messiah would pour out/give His life *for many* (recall that in Hebrew *many* is an inclusive word that virtually means "all"). **Mark 10:45** says that His life would be a ransom. **Isaiah 53:12** says that His life would be poured out in death and that He would bear the sin of many. Jesus' words point forward to the wedding banquet that He will celebrate with His people (His bride) when the kingdom is consummated.

4. The striking of the shepherd and the scattering of the disciples were a part of God's action to make for Himself a purified people who would trust in Him as their God. Jesus assured His disciples that He would rise from the dead and go ahead of them to Galilee where the scattered sheep would be regathered. Loyalty, love, and faith were obviously behind Peter's declaration, but He also showed no understanding of his own weakness. He apparently also did not understand Jesus' declaration that He would rise

from the dead. Note that according to tradition Peter eventually did lose his life because of his association with Jesus.

5. Jesus watched (was spiritually alert) and communed with His Father in prayer. He encouraged the disciples to do the same for He knew that they, like all people except Himself, were weak, sinful, and prone to fall into temptation. Their only hope against temptation lay with God and the willing spirit that He granted to His people to sustain them **(Psalm 51:11–12)**.

6. The cup was the cup of God's wrath against the sin of all humanity. Jesus was about to drink it for all people. Drinking that cup would alienate Jesus from His Father, the prospect of which filled Him with distress. Jesus addressed God with *Abba*, a familiar, everyday term for *father* that is similar to our term *daddy*. Jews in Jesus' day did not use that term for God and would have considered its use disrespectful. But by using it Jesus showed His intimate relationship with His Father. Jesus showed His obedient submission by asking that the Father accomplish His will, not Jesus' will. Jesus' words in **14:42** indicate a willingness to go and meet those who were approaching to arrest Him, thus submitting Himself to the evident will of His Father.

7. Throughout His ministry, Jesus had kept His identity a closely guarded secret to avoid stirring up the false popular expectations of the Messiah. Now He responded that indeed He was the Messiah and that these men would see the proof when they saw Him sitting at the right hand of God and coming on the clouds of heaven. The Sanhedrin took this as an affront to the majesty and authority of God and condemned Jesus for blasphemy. They then repudiated any involvement in His supposed blasphemy by spitting on and hitting Him. They also taunted Him to prove that He was the Messiah by prophesying who hit Him while He was blindfolded.

8. Fearful of the derision of his challengers and the possible consequences of being associated with Jesus, Peter denied any involvement with Him. When the cock crowed the second time, it jogged Peter's memory of how Jesus had predicted exactly what he was now doing. Peter was overcome with grief and shame.

The Word for Us

1. Like Peter, all of us are weak and sinful and susceptible to temptation. We ought to recognize this and never become confident of our own ability to stand up for Jesus when we are threatened. Instead, we ought to obey Jesus' words to watch (be spiritually alert) and pray because reliance on the power and help of God is our only hope in the face of Satan's temptations, which seek to separate us from our Lord. If Jesus watched and

prayed in the hour of darkness, should we do any less? The petitions "Thy will be done," "lead us not into temptation," and "deliver us from evil" are particularly applicable when we are persecuted and tempted to deny our Lord. Of course we pray that persecution and temptation end, yet like Jesus we should ask the Lord to accomplish His will, not our own, even if that means we continue to suffer. But we can do so, knowing that the Lord Jesus has not abandoned us but that He is with us to strengthen and uphold us. In the Lord's Supper He assures us of His continual presence with us and provides us with the forgiveness that His broken body and shed blood won for us. Such assurance strengthens our faith.

2. Rejection, ridicule, and death for the sake of Jesus should surprise no Christian. Answers will vary. In some countries today Christians do face physical persecution and death because of their faith in Jesus. In others like our own, their beliefs and values are reviled and desecrated by the media and by popular culture.

Closing

Sing or speak together "The Death of Jesus Christ, Our Lord."

To Do This Week

Urge participants to complete the suggested activity prior to the next class session.

Lesson 10

Jesus Is Crucified and Rises from the Dead

Theme Verse

Read aloud the theme verse.

Goal

Invite a volunteer to read aloud the goal.

What's Going On Here?

Read aloud and discuss briefly the introductory paragraph.

Searching the Scriptures

1. Jesus told Pilate that His kingdom was not of this world, but from another place (from heaven).

2. Jesus knew that it was His Father's will for Him to suffer and die, and He obediently submitted to that will. Note again the fulfillment of **Isaiah 53:7.** Pilate was amazed at His silence, undoubtedly because he was used to people in that situation desperately trying to defend themselves and escape punishment.

3. Seeking some entertainment, the soldiers mocked Jesus' kingship by dressing Him in a purple robe and crown of thorns, pretending to pay Him homage, spitting on Him, and hitting Him on the head.

4. Jesus chose to endure the suffering appointed for Him in full consciousness.

5. Jesus was reviled by those who passed by, by the religious leaders, and by the men who were crucified with Him (one of these men changed his mind; see **Luke 23:39–43**). The cruel mockery, including the shaking of heads was prophesied, as was the content of the insults (compare **Psalm 22:8** with **Matt. 27:41–43**), the effects of crucifixion on the body, the piercing of the hands and feet, the encirclement by enemies, the stares from bystanders, and the division of clothing by lots. It was a common Roman practice for those performing an execution to divide up the victims' minor possessions.

6. Sin separates people from God who is holy. Jesus was alienated from His Father on the cross because He was bearing the consequences of sin for all people. Jesus' form of address ("My God") show that He still had faith in His Father.

7. The tearing of the curtain signified that God had accepted in full Jesus' sacrifice on behalf of all people, that all the barriers between God and people had been removed, that the sacrificial system had accomplished its purpose and was no longer necessary, and that all people now have access to God through Jesus.

8. The centurion confessed that Jesus was the Son of God.

9. The angel made clear that the man who had risen was Jesus of Nazareth, who had been crucified. Resurrection is totally outside of human experience, and without the explanation of the angel, all that would be evident to people was that the body was no longer in the tomb.

10. Peter was specifically mentioned so that he would know that he was forgiven and would not be excluded because of his denial of Jesus. Recall that Jesus' prediction that He would meet His disciples in Galilee after His resurrection occurred at the same time when He predicted that they would all desert Him **(14:27–28).** All of the disciples would have been comforted

by the fact that Jesus was going to restore them to fellowship with Himself despite their desertion of Him.

11. The women's experience parallels that of Peter, James, and John at the transfiguration. When people are confronted by the direct activity of God, their first reaction is fear.

> Those who are confronted with God's direct intervention in the historical process do not know how to react. Divine revelation lies beyond normal human experience, and there are no categories available to men which enable them to understand and respond appropriately. The first human response is overwhelming fear (William L. Lane, *The Gospel of Mark*, The New International Commentary on the New Testament [Grand Rapids, MI: Eerdmans, 1974], p. 590).

12. The disciples were commanded to preach the Gospel throughout the world. Those who believe the Gospel and are baptized will be saved. Those who do not believe will be condemned. Note that lack of Baptism does not damn those who have faith, but it is assumed that those who have faith have been baptized.

The Word for Us

1. Jesus' crucifixion and resurrection are central to the church's life and teaching because only here has God mercifully dealt with the problem of human enslavement to sin, Satan, and death. Throughout His life, but especially in going to the cross, Jesus submitted Himself to God's will, something no one else since Adam has been able to do perfectly. This obedience is transferred to the account of all who have faith in Jesus. On the cross, Jesus bore the punishment that all people deserve by their sin and won the decisive victory against Satan and his forces. Jesus made it possible for people who had been alienated from God by their sin to be reconciled to Him. The resurrection showed that death, the ultimate punishment for sin, could not hold Jesus and would not hold those who put their trust in Him. Answers will vary. An overemphasis on keeping the Law and on sanctification sometimes overshadows the Gospel. An overemphasis on making this world a better place to live also at times overshadows the Gospel.

2. Answers may vary. All of our debts to God were paid by Jesus on the cross. We now have access to and fellowship with our Creator. Jesus' resurrection insures us that we too will rise to new life after we die, new life that will be lived in unending fellowship with God in a place where there is no more sin or death or evil or pain or alienation (see **1 Cor. 15:20–23; Rev. 21:1–7**).

3. Answers may vary. We participate in the spread of the Gospel as we witness, as we pray, and as we support other Christians in their ministry through financial gifts and encouragement.

Closing

Speak or sing together "Oh, Love, How Deep."